THE
ALL-ROUND
ACTIVITY BOOK

GET CREATIVE WITH ACTIVITIES,
GAMES AND ILLUSIONS
ALL BASED ON DOTS

PATRICIA MOFFETT

CARLTON
BOOKS

In memory of the blue border collie
Pinky Marvin, who is no longer assisting
at my feet.

THIS IS A CARLTON BOOK

Published by Carlton Books Ltd

20 Mortimer Street

London W1T 3JW

Copyright © Carlton Publishing Group
2019

A CIP catalogue for this book is available
from the British Library.

Editorial Manager: Chris Mitchell

Design Manager: Luke Griffin

Production: Jessica Arvidsson

ISBN 978-1-78739-111-6

Printed in China

10 9 8 7 6 5 4 3 2 1

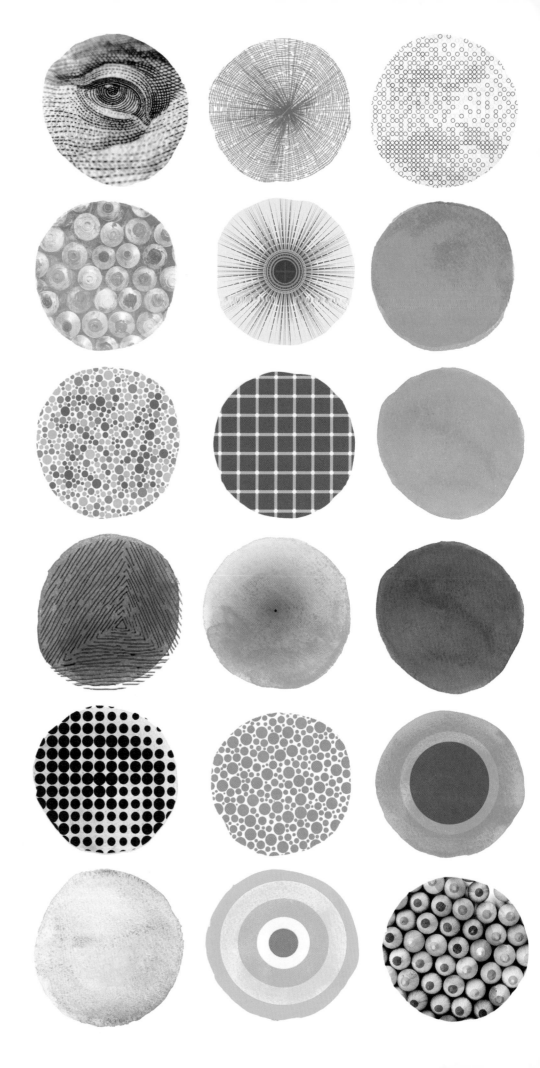

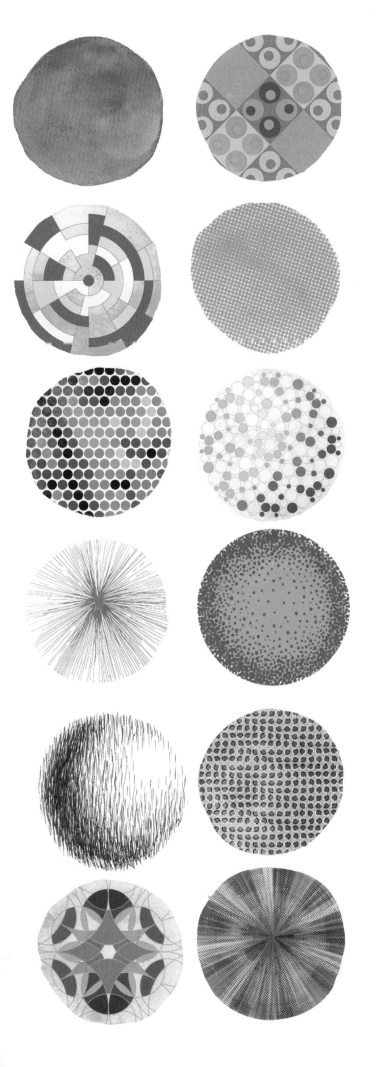

Contents

Foreword 4

Introduction 6

Circles and Colour 16

Grey Areas 28

Circular Codes 36

Deceptive Dots 42

Dot Playground 54

Dot Maths 74

Solutions 91

The Importance of Dots

It is often the little things that are the basis of progress... So let me tell you a little story about the tiniest thing on earth: the dot.

Thousands of years ago, a man in his solitude scanned the night sky and saw all those dots shining like so many still fireflies and, perhaps for fun, he decided to join them together to form shapes. This is how zodiac signs and astronomy were born.

Far away, in ancient India, the dot symbolized beauty and the eye of knowledge. But even more, the dot they called "shunya-bindu" represented what we nowadays know as zero. It was first a placeholder and then a fully fledged number, for when it is added to the right of the representation of any given digit, the value of the digit is multiplied by ten. This is how our current numbers and decimal numeration system were born.

While drawing or painting, visual artists of all times used to fix a dot - or more specifically a point in space - which was traditionally visualized from the tip of their thumb. Eventually, when this point receded so far away in space, it became known as a "vanishing point". A vanishing point is where all converging lines of a landscape meet at the horizon. This is how perspective and geometry were born.

One day, medieval musicians were tired of having to rely solely on their memories to remember songs. So they started to use dots, named "puncti", placed on or between four lines to represent the pitch and duration of a sound. This is how musical notation and programming were born.

In the modern era, at the beginning of the nineteenth century, dots were used in many other symbolic forms: bumps, holes, single tones, flashes of light... Do the terms Braille, Morse, punched card or pixel sound familiar to you? This is how communication and coding were born.

I could go on forever listing all the fascinating properties and curiosities regarding dots, but I don't want to spoil your pleasure in discovering the many applications in everyday life and other funny interactive activities this intriguing book offers.

As an optical-art expert, I am pleased that this work also contains a neat collection of optical illusions that will encourage the reader to further explore the compelling world of visual perception. You will be surprised at how, through puzzles, games and art activities, this "dot workshop" will afford insight into the perceptual and conceptual beauty of science and nature.

The author of this volume, Patricia Moffett, is known for her beautifully illustrated colouring and activity books featuring detailed figures and fabulous characters amidst fairy worlds.

Don't wait any more, go and immerse yourself in this captivating "dot experience".

Oh wait, just one more word... I almost forgot to say that this book also conveys a philosophical message as it reminds us that we will always be a "dot" to someone or something else: a flea is a dot compared to a man, a man is a dot compared to the earth, the earth is a blue dot compared to the sun, the sun is one of those dots in the Milky Way and our galaxy is a dot in the universe. That's all from me. I will sign off with another dot... a full stop! Enjoy.

Gianni A. Sarcone
Artist & Visual Researcher

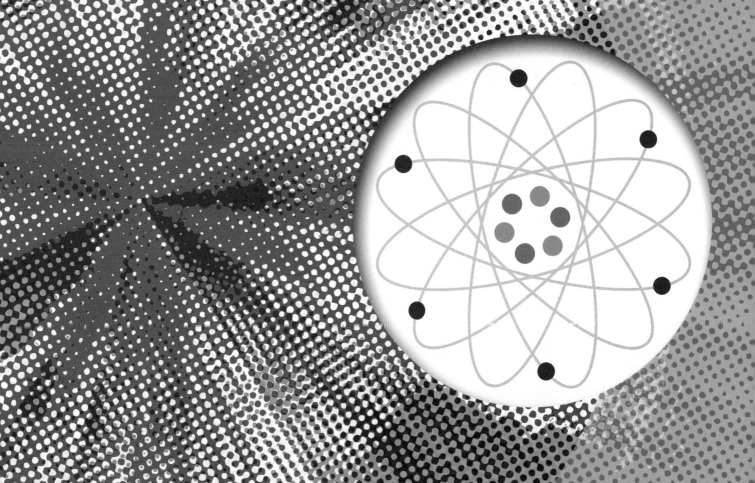

Introduction

Introduction
Welcome to *The All-Round Activity Book*!

This book is full of activities, puzzles and fascinating things all with a circular theme...

... you'll work with dots in pictures, circular codes, dot maths, deceptive dots, and most fun of all, dot playgrounds!

Throughout the sections there are pages themed as:

PUZZLE

Mazes, maths and observation puzzles

MAKE IT

Cut-out objects to be constructed

ART QUEST

A challenging creative exercise thinking about colour, tone or form

OPTICAL ILLUSION

Let your eyes deceive you into seeing wriggling pages or vibrant after-images

COLOUR IN

Follow a suggested scheme to reveal a mosaic picture

ACTIVITY

No right or wrong answer, just some fun stuff to while away the time enjoyably

It Started with a Sphere

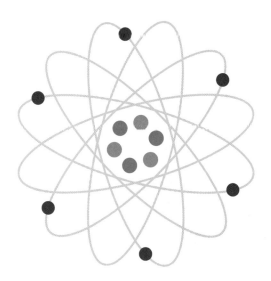

Dots are the building blocks of everything.

The word atom comes from the Greek word atomos and it means indivisible. Demokritos, the Greek philosopher, visualized an atom as a sphere... a dot at the very root of everything!

Atomic theory developed in the 18th century to include ideas about elements and molecules, and later that the atom itself was made up of the smaller particles of a nucleus and electrons. We continued to visualize these as sets of spheres until, in the early 21st century, we were able to produce actual images of atoms.

Above: *Atomic structure of a platinum crystal with many facets, some of them resolved to show single atoms.*

Left: *How we have come to visualize atoms.*

Dotting the Eyes

Back in the world that's visible to our naked eyes, we can analyse then recreate images for reproduction using dots. Lets start by taking a look at how tone is printed.

Above: *Close up detail of the engraving of Benjamin Franklin on a $100 bill.*

Setting the Tone - matters of size

Before modern printing processes, images were made for reproduction by engraving and etching onto metal plates.

Artists working through this medium often print images with just black ink and draw the lines they engrave in a way that suggests tone.

These lines were faded-out by breaking them up into ever-smaller dots so that, when seen from a distance, they read as shades of grey.

In the books and newspapers we read today, images that have continuous-tone are analysed by mechanical means before being printed. The darkness of the grey is represented by the size of the dot that is printed - the lighter the area represented, the smaller the dot.

The artist also has the option to draw lines that follow the contours of the subject matter - this gives further information to the viewer as to the form of the subject.

Left: *Close up of part of a mechanical halftone.*

Setting the Tone
– dim and dimmer

How do we see greys on media where the pixels are a fixed size?

Here, shades are represented by dimming or brightening each pixel. The number of steps in grey shades depend on what is called *bit depth*. Initially in 1 bit, black and white, the pixels are either on or off. Increases in bit depths now mean that monitors can display tens of throusands of grey shades.

We'll be trying a similar effect on page 30.

Above: *Pixelated grey image showing how each pixel is cranked up or down to read as a tonal image.*

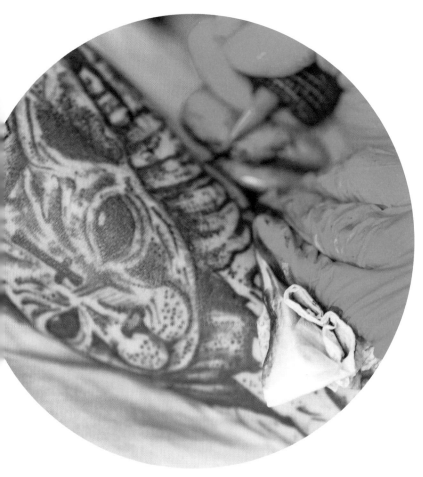

Above: *A black-only tattoo that has form expressed by the density of the dots.*

Setting the Tone
– crowd control

Think of a tattoo that's just drawn with black ink - any tonal areas are suggested by using dots of black. Whilst there are needles of different sizes available, they're not comparable to the infinitely variable size of half-tone dots.

So what other variable do we have at our disposal?

Density: how many dots there are in a given area - lots in the deepest shades and fewer in the lighter areas.

Try this out in the activities on pages 24 and 25.

Mixed Colours

Look up close at a colour print. Advertising billboards are great for this. Notice that the array of colours you see are made from dots of just four colours. The same is true of a monitor or TV screen... three colours there – but why are the colours different in each?

Reflected light (light bounced off objects such as paint on paper) and *projected light* (light we look at straight from its source such as an LED) have different primary colours. The primary colours of *reflected light* are red, yellow and blue. The primary colours of *projected light* are red, green and blue.

So why don't printed images use red, yellow and blue? What's the pink and turquoisey blue about?

The colours we use for print – cyan, magenta, yellow and black (CMYK) – are, in fact, slightly murkier versions of the secondary colours of light. It's all to do with how the images are analysed to find out how the colours are made up. Black is added to give extra richness and depth to the darker tones.

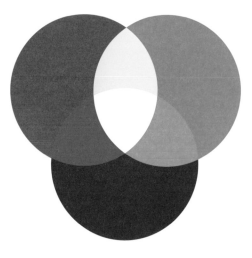

Above: *The circles are coloured in the primary colours of light: red, green and blue (RGB). The overlapping of these, when light is projected, makes more light: brighter colours!*

We can see that these lighter, brighter secondary colours are magenta, yellow and cyan.

Left: *Mixing the secondary colours of light as printed dots. These dots, when they overlap, darken and mix to make shades to nearly black (CMYK).*

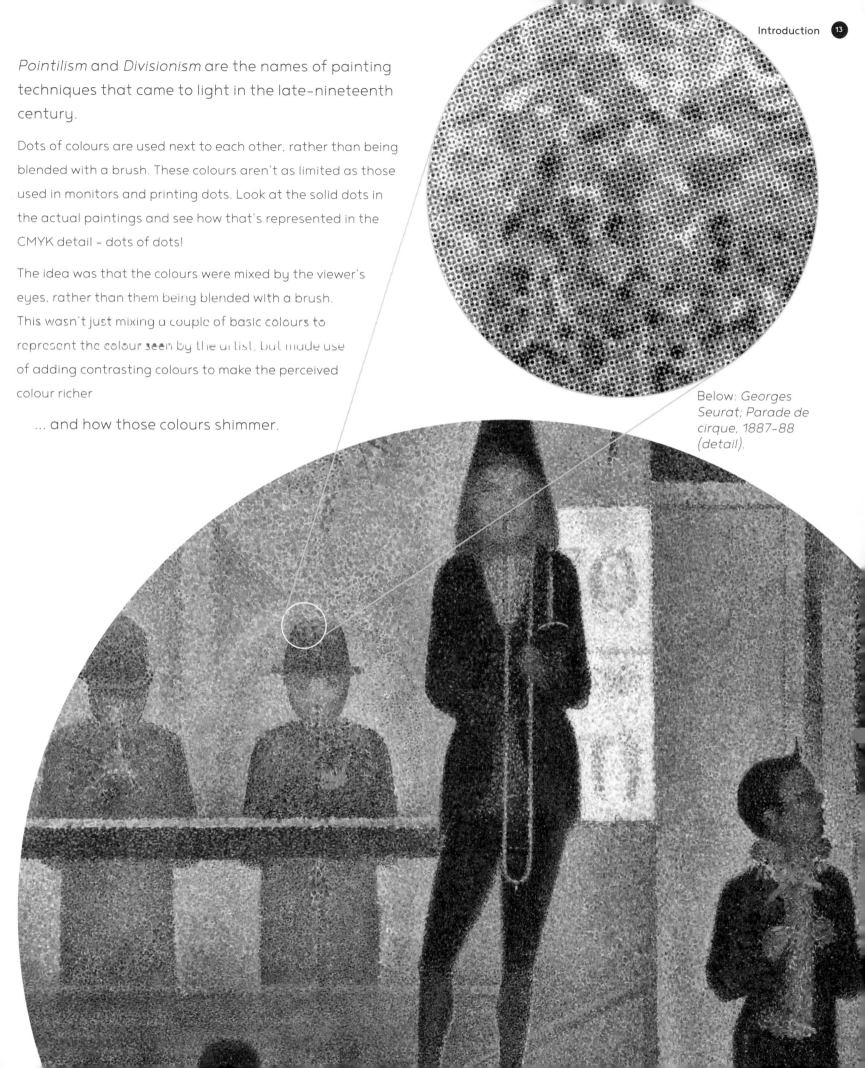

Pointilism and *Divisionism* are the names of painting techniques that came to light in the late-nineteenth century.

Dots of colours are used next to each other, rather than being blended with a brush. These colours aren't as limited as those used in monitors and printing dots. Look at the solid dots in the actual paintings and see how that's represented in the CMYK detail - dots of dots!

The idea was that the colours were mixed by the viewer's eyes, rather than them being blended with a brush. This wasn't just mixing a couple of basic colours to represent the colour seen by the artist, but made use of adding contrasting colours to make the perceived colour richer

... and how those colours shimmer.

Below: *Georges Seurat; Parade de cirque, 1887-88 (detail).*

Breaking Up!

Just as dots can help to describe form, they can also help to disguise it.

Many animals are dotted or speckled to break up the solidity of their shape... dark dots at the edge of their silhouette might merge with a dark patch of landscape to make their outline less recognizable to prey and predators.

Above: Notice how the dots on this bird's plumage help it to blend in to the background.

Left: Chameleons take this way too far with their colour-changing, dot-encrusted skin
... where DID I put that lizard?

Packed in Tight

Think of a dot in 3D and you have a sphere – and bubbles can be fun-to-play-with spheres!

When the surface tension of a film of soap snaps around a pocket of air, the shape it forms is a sphere. Coincidentally, a sphere is the shape with the smallest surface-area-to-volume ratio,

All-Round Senses

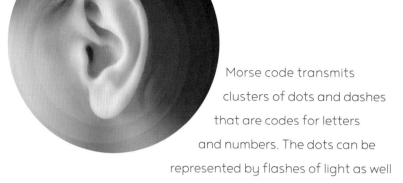

If we think of the word dot, in our minds we usually SEE a dot.... but dots can be read by our ears or by touch.

Letters of an alphabet can be felt as raised dots in Braille or heard as bursts of sound in Morse code.

Braille uses a matrix of six dots, in two columns of three. Letters and words are read feeling the combinations of raised dots. Braille products are made with a special typewriting machine with six keys. Each key corresponds to one of the dots in the matrix.

Morse code transmits clusters of dots and dashes that are codes for letters and numbers. The dots can be represented by flashes of light as well as by sound. Weirdly enough, you can speak Morse code – dots are "di", except when they are the last one in a sequence – then they are "dit". Dashes are spoken as "dah".

Check out the activity on page 32.

Computer Love

Believe it or not, there are three paper computer programs that are run by dots!

As early as 1725, a way of controlling the threads on looms with punchcards was invented. The dot holes in the card controlled the mixing of the threads to produce beautiful and intricate patterns.

An automated piano, a pianola, can play tunes that are driven by rolls of paper programs. The position of the dots across the roll dictates which key is pressed. The distance up or down controls when.

Towards the middle of the last century, the way to input data into computers was through dots punched in strips of paper. The smaller dots down the centre act as sprocket holes to feed the paper along, and the larger dots on either side are the actual binary data.

And this type of technology is still inspiring people. *Wintergaten*, the Swedish folktronika band, have invented some hugely entertaining music machines, including ones run by punchtape.

What will dots do for you? I'd love to know.

Have fun!
Patricia Moffett

Circles and Colour

**ART
QUEST**

Colour Circles

Colour in the circles on the opposite page. There are many ways to combine areas to make new shapes . You could explore the six-fold symmetry and make snowflakes and patterns or make more organic shapes.

ACTIVITY

Ishihara Tests

These tests were devised by Dr Shinobu Ishihara in 1917. The dots make use of subtle variations in hue and shade to reveal the type of colour-vision anomalies a person has.

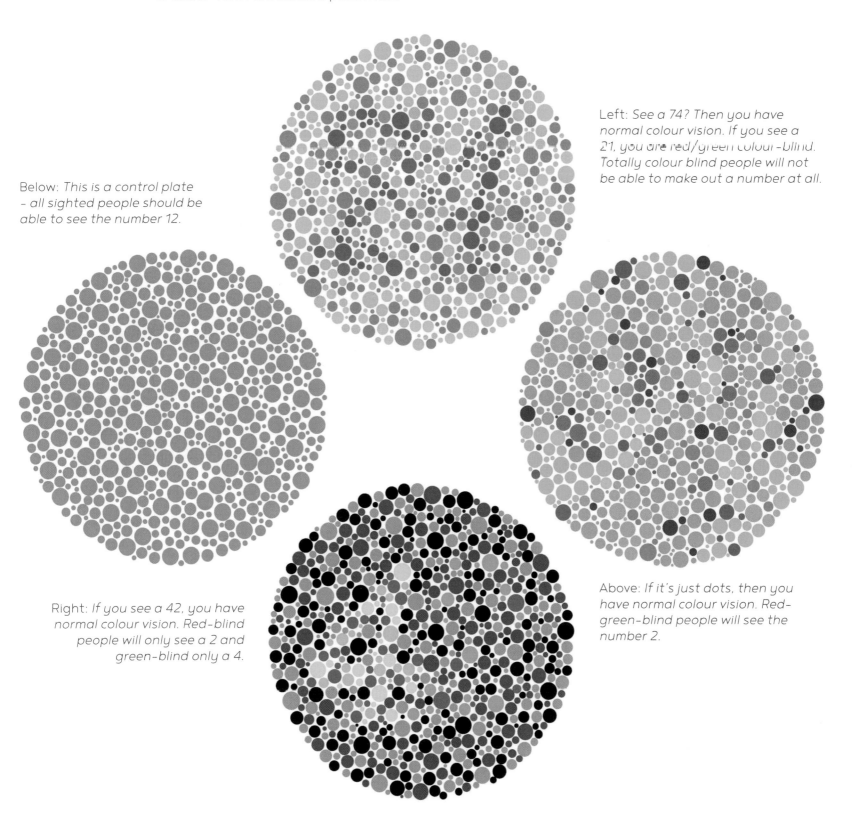

Left: See a 74? Then you have normal colour vision. If you see a 21, you are red/green colour-blind. Totally colour blind people will not be able to make out a number at all.

Below: This is a control plate - all sighted people should be able to see the number 12.

Right: If you see a 42, you have normal colour vision. Red-blind people will only see a 2 and green-blind only a 4.

Above: If it's just dots, then you have normal colour vision. Red-green-blind people will see the number 2.

OPTICAL ILLUSION

After Image

Stare at the black dot below for at least 60 seconds. Then look at the white page to the right. The true colours and light values of the image should be seen.

Because the image was negative to start with, it appears correctly as an after image.

ART QUEST

Colour Wheel

Here is a partially completed colour wheel - complete the wheel by colouring in the white circles. Try using coloured pencils and build up each circle gradually. When you're done, half close your eyes - the transitions should be smooth without any jumps. It's harder than it looks to balance the whole circle. If you get stuck, have a look at the solution on page 92.

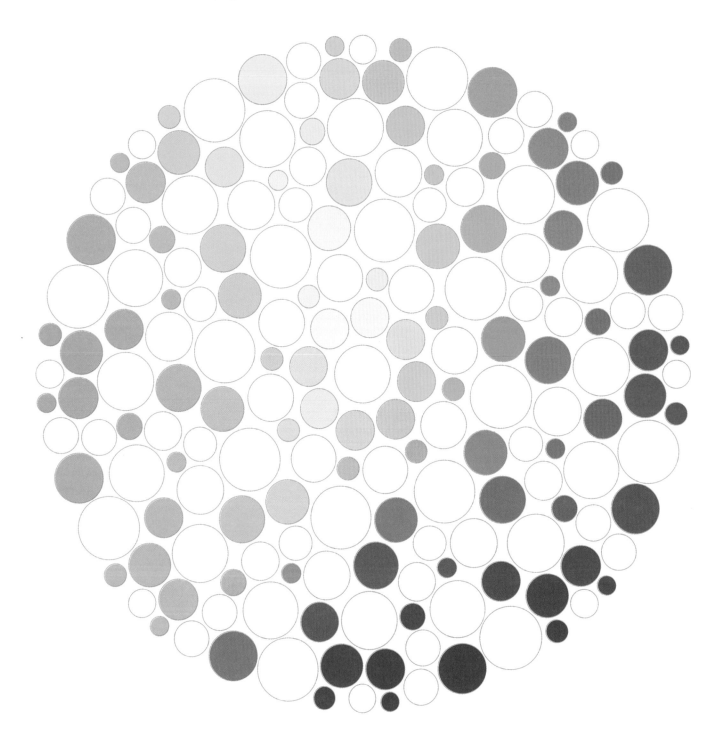

Colour Notes: *Hues are changes in colour as light moves through the spectrum. Hues revolve around the circle like a clock.*

In our wheel, white is added to the hues to make tints that get paler towards the centre.

COLOUR IN

Stand Well Back!

Colour the circles the same colour as their outlines. Up close, we can see what the image is, but the colours look really strange. Stand well back and watch the image blend.

Flashing Colour

Some colours, when placed next to each other, seem to flash – these are usually saturated colours that sit opposite each other on the colour wheel. If you've studied page 24, you'll know what this means. Either way – time to wear shades!

Grey Areas

ART QUEST

Dotting Tones

In the same way that a tattooist suggests tone, shade the blank shapes using just black dots made with a pen. This technique is called stippling – here's the idea on the right.

Ready for more? Shade this design using black dots with a pen. This time it's up to you to decide how the tones work. Have a good think about it – you don't have to treat each element the same each time it appears. Maybe the whole image will get darker or lighter from top to bottom. Consider adding dotted pattern as well as tone.

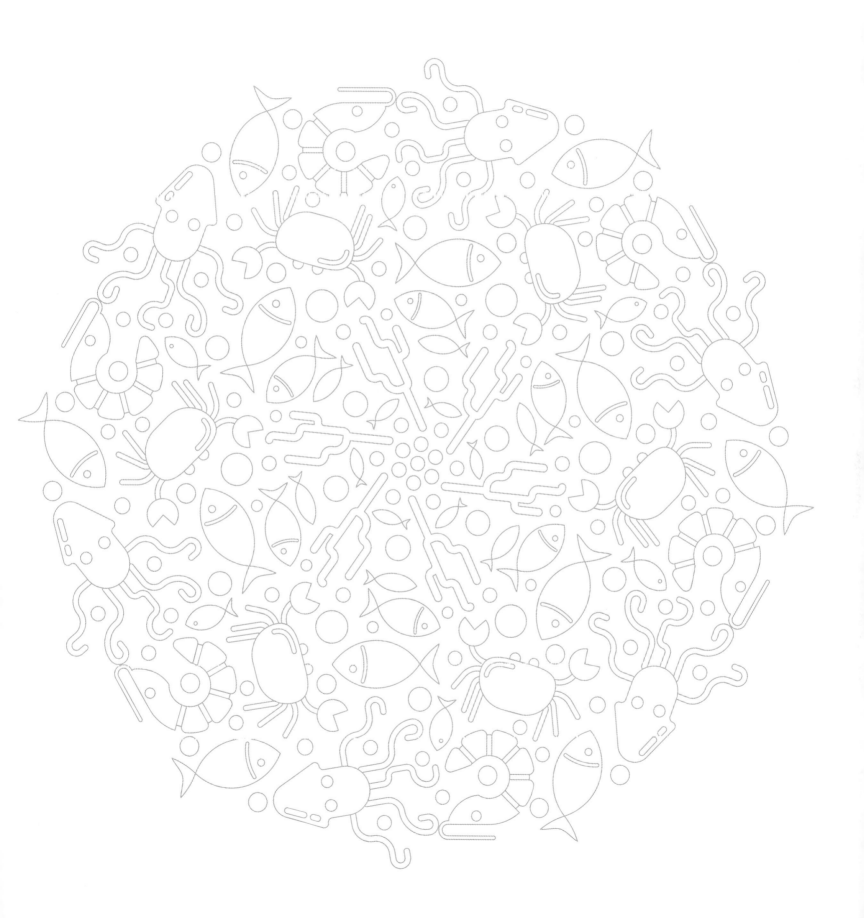

PUZZLE

Clean up on page 32!

Stare at the black dot. In a short time the grey tone around it will start to disappear. If only all clean-ups were this easy!

•

OPTICAL ILLUSION

Spot who?

Stand well back. See if you recognize the face in these dots. All is revealed on page 86.

Grey Days

Grey, rainy days... Dots of drops cover the window.

Look very closely and see how each one is an upside-down reflection of the scene outside.

COLOUR IN

Cloud Tones

Make a moody sky with these dotty clouds... take a 2B pencil and colour in the white centre of each dot until it matches the line around it. Look carefully, some lines are very pale, but none are white... you'll need the lightest touch for these. Completed image on page 92.

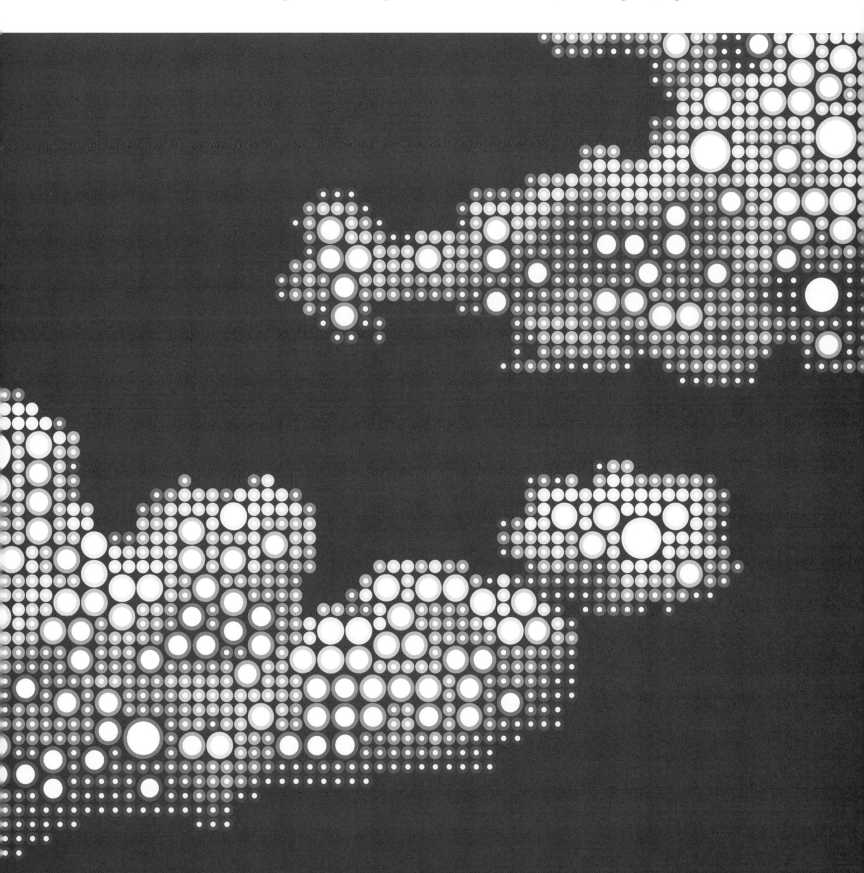

Circular Codes

Coded Numbers

Here's a chart with numbers from 0-9 as Morse code, binary and Braille.

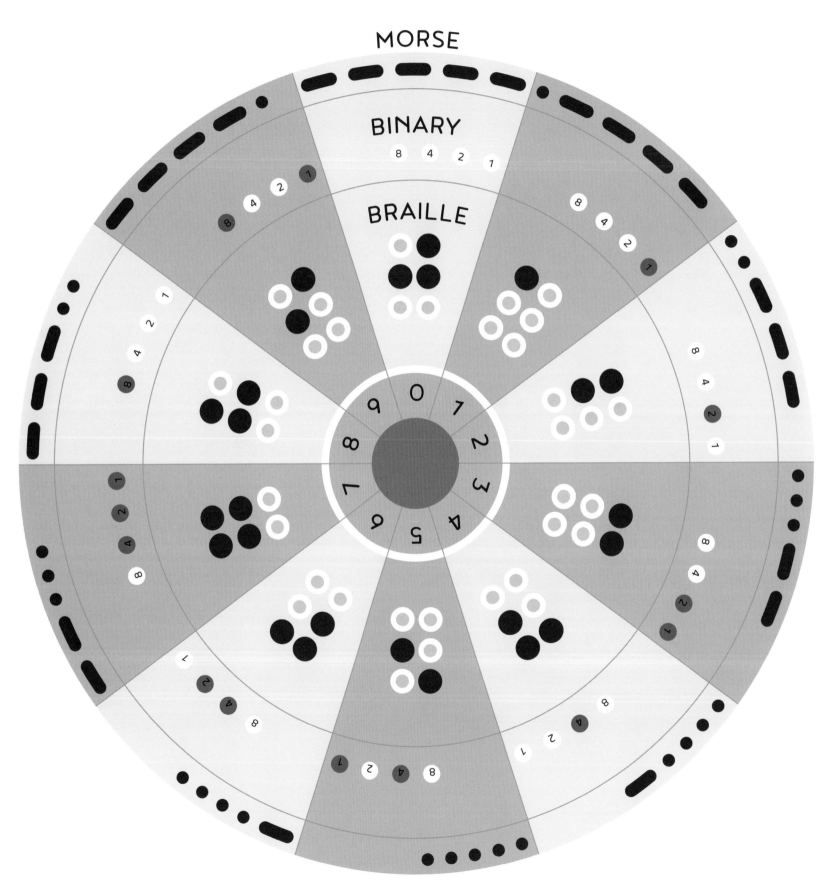

Think of a number – a special date. Colour it in one, or all, of the codes on the grid of dots below. It could be a date of birth or another important day. To make the dashes of Morse code, join three dots together in a row. Leave three dot spaces between each Morse code number. Once you've designed with this grid, copy it and make a card or a framed graphic picture.

PUZZLE

Circular Logic

Here are some puzzles that will tax your non-verbal reasoning skills. Work out which dot or dollection of dots is missing from the grids. Crack the code to open the padlock.

The solutions are on page 92.

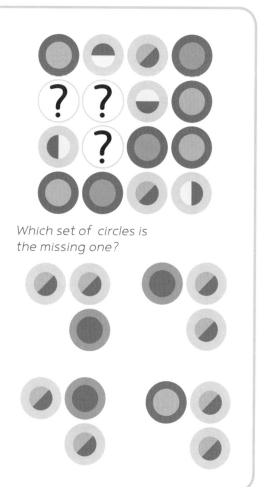

Which set of circles is the missing one?

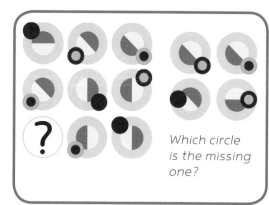

Which circle is the missing one?

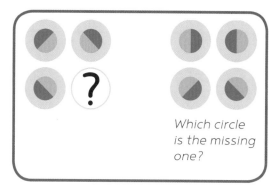

Which circle is the missing one?

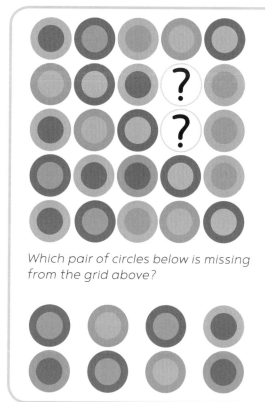

Which pair of circles below is missing from the grid above?

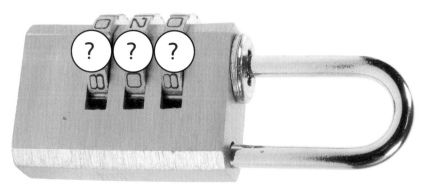

Read the clues next to each set of circles and work out which combination of circles will open the lock.

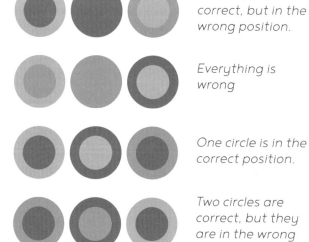

One circle is correct, but in the wrong position.

Everything is wrong

One circle is in the correct position.

Two circles are correct, but they are in the wrong position

One circle is correct, but in the wrong position.

Numberless Dot2Dot

PUZZLE

Study the code. Notice how the ringed dots only appear once per loop and how certain coloured dots connect to the outer ring.

Code: Follow the logic and make a star. If you get stuck, the solution is on page 93.

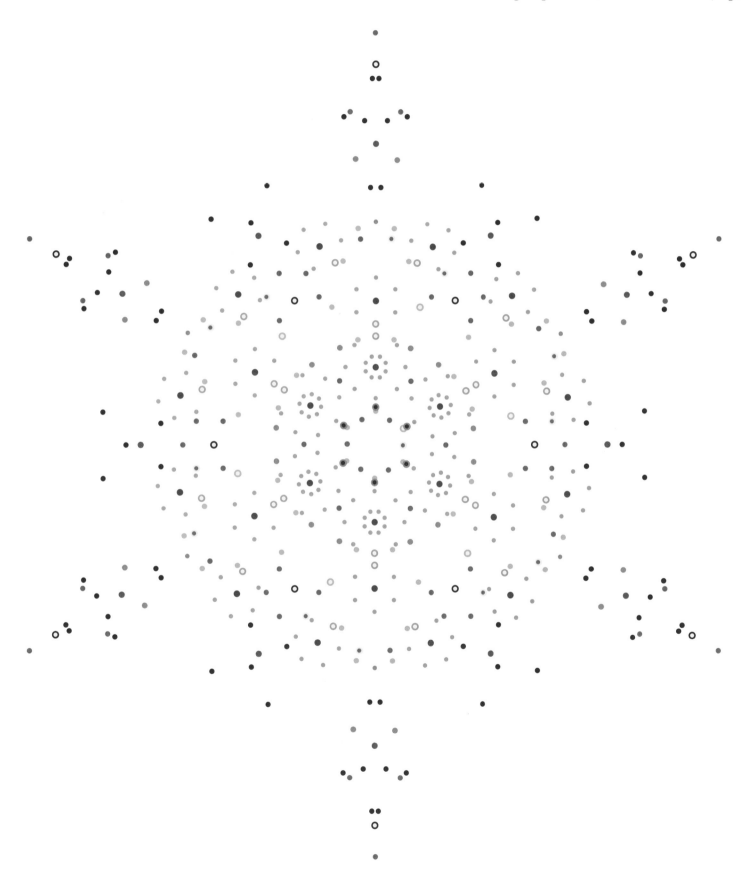

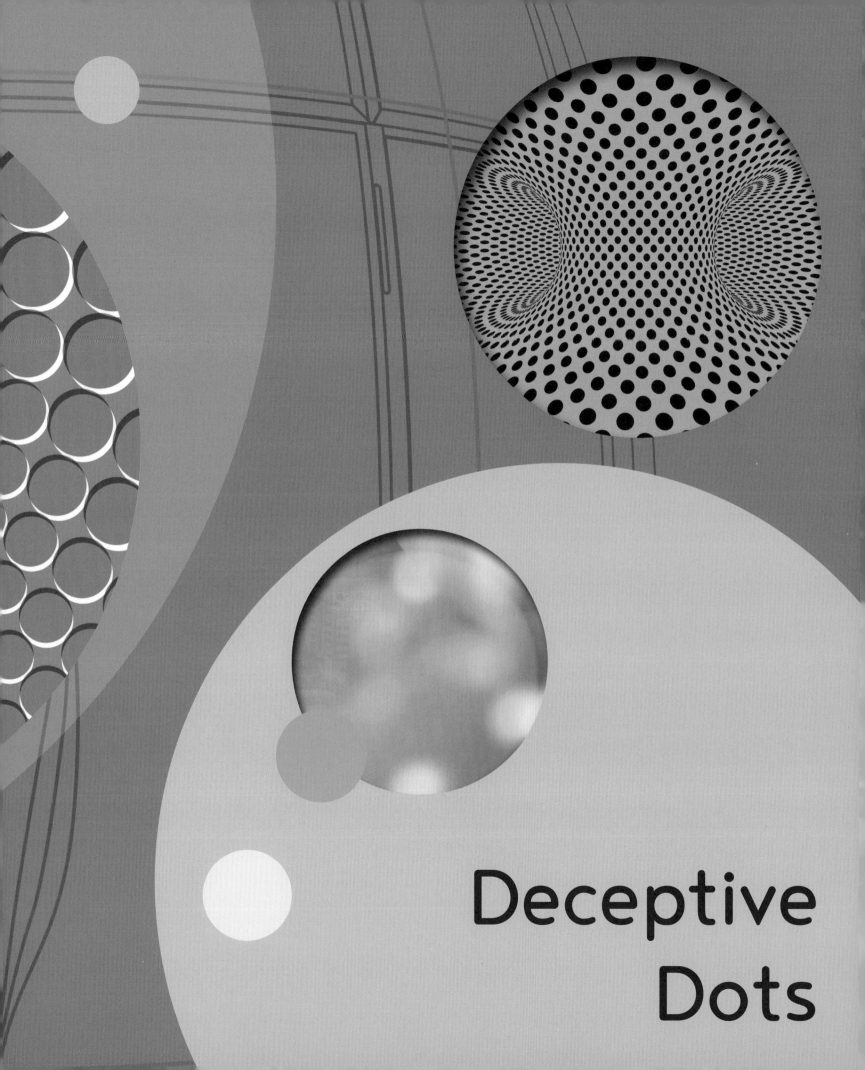

Deceptive
Dots

Bokeh

Have you noticed that lots of photographs have big soft dots in them? This is called Bokeh, or Boke, and is the Japanese word for "blur".

Cameras can be set up to focus at a certain distance and not much beyond or in front. Therefore, all other distances will be out of focus and blurry. Many high-quality lenses have smooth, rounded apertures that capture these out-of-focus areas as circles. The higher the contrast of light and dark, the more prominent the circles appear. Notice how most of the big soft dots you see in this type of photograph are lights or reflections.

**ART
QUEST**

Spherical Scene

Fish-eye lenses and convex mirrors produce intriguing distortions. Artists
as far back as Van Eyck in the 15th century have been fascinated with them.

Use the blue grids to guide you in mapping this interior on to a sphere. Some parts have already been plotted to start you off.

If you get in a pickle, the completed drawing can be seen on page 93.

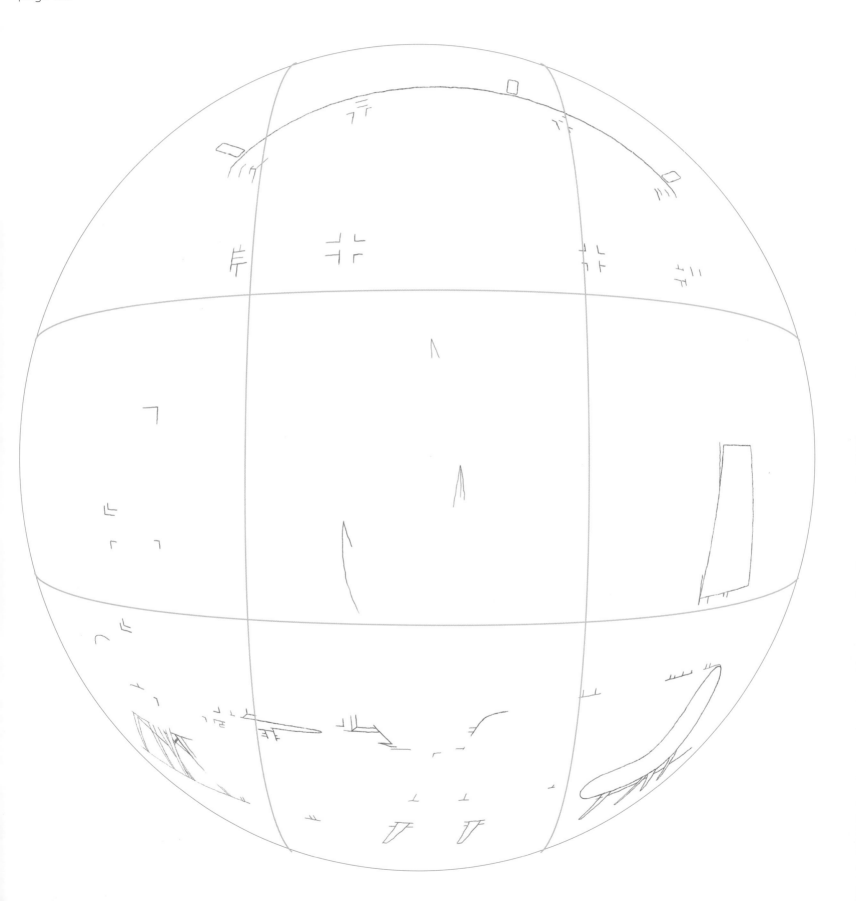

OPTICAL ILLUSION

Shy Dark Dots

Chase the darker dots with your eyes. See how they jump out of the way.

Was it something you said?

Colour Me Kahlo

Dig out your coloured pencils and match the ten colours below as closely as possible. Colour each circle according to the number in it. Stand back and see who you've got! You can see a completed example on page 94.

COLOUR IN

**OPTICAL
ILLUSION**

It Lives!

The theory behind this crazy optical effect is uncertain...

Somehow your motion sensors are getting confused by what you see.

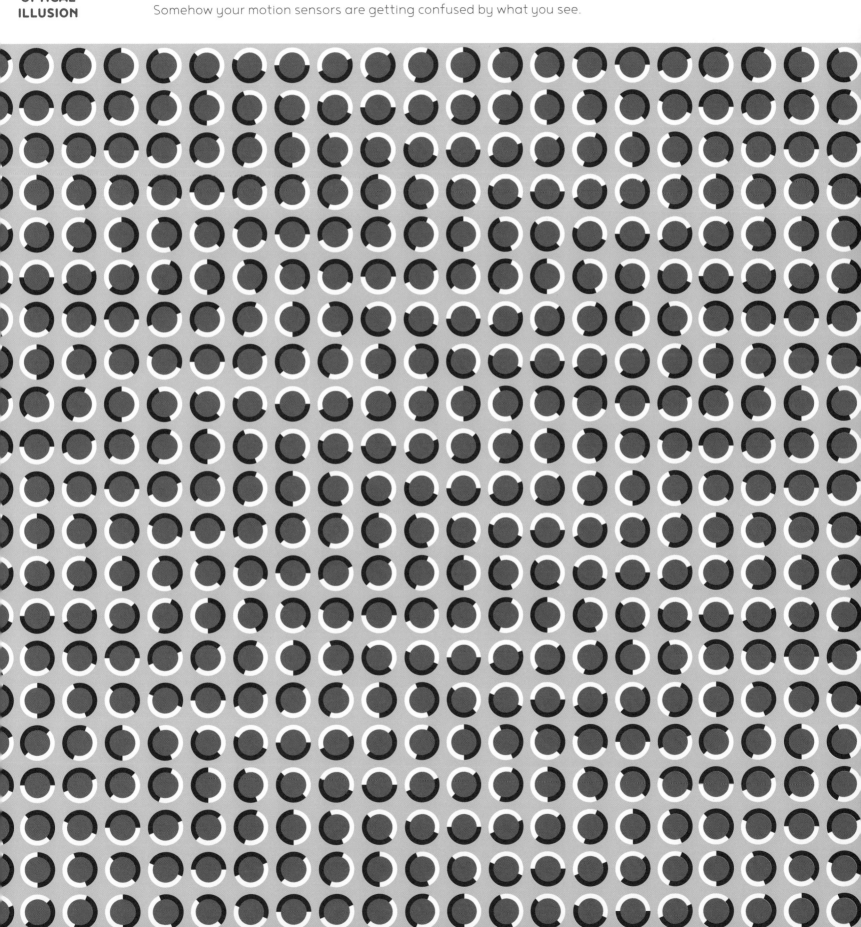

The Original Dot to Dots

The Ancients gazed up at the night sky and imagined the dots of stars forming images.

Different cultures joined the dots in different ways, resulting in their own interpretations and associated stories. Here are the constellations that represent the signs of the zodiac from Greek mythology – can you work out which ones are which?

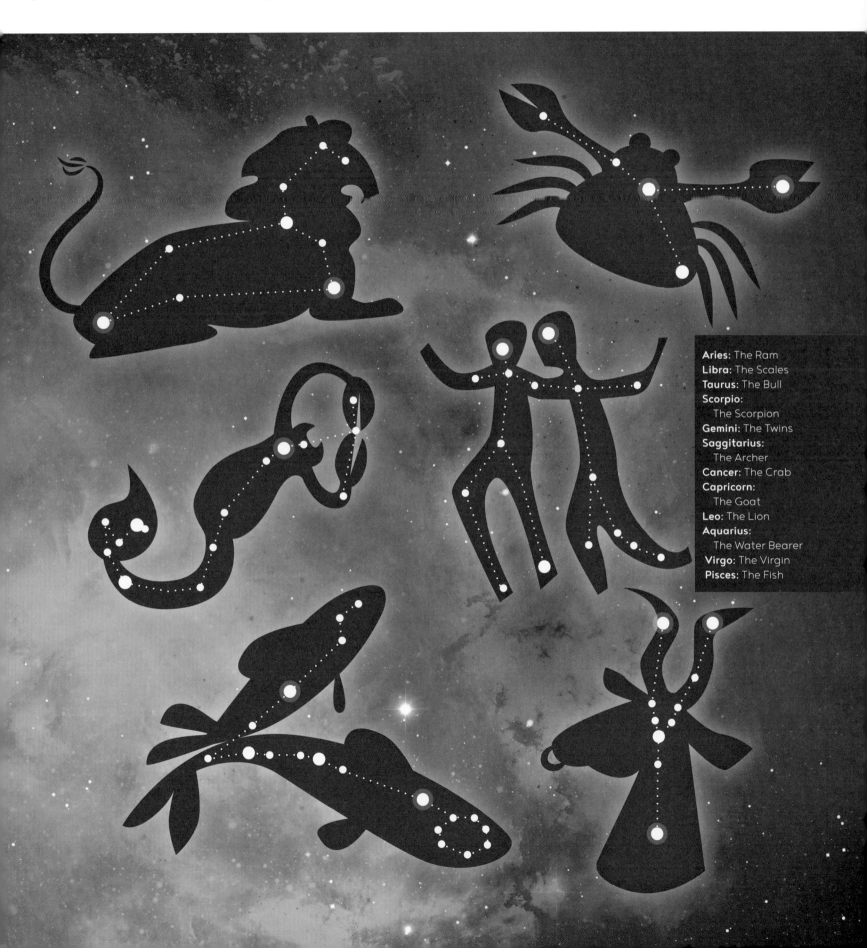

Aries: The Ram
Libra: The Scales
Taurus: The Bull
Scorpio:
    The Scorpion
Gemini: The Twins
Saggitarius:
    The Archer
Cancer: The Crab
Capricorn:
    The Goat
Leo: The Lion
Aquarius:
    The Water Bearer
Virgo: The Virgin
Pisces: The Fish

Dot
Playground

Eye Spy

What's going on here? Do people say you're always making something out of nothing? Have a go at adding something to the circles on this page...

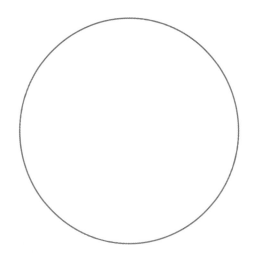
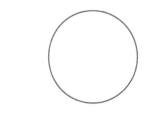
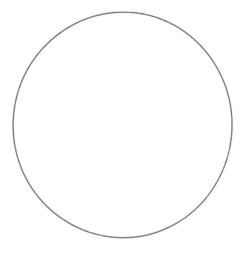
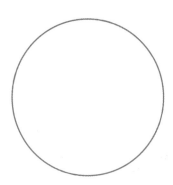
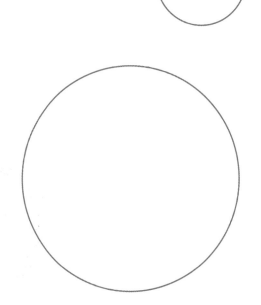
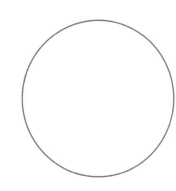

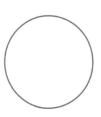
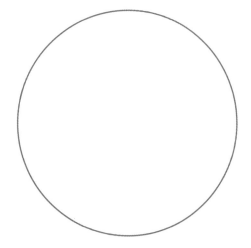

What I saw through the telescope

MAKE IT

FlexiDots

A flexagon is made by folding a strip of equilateral triangles to form a hexagon.

This is then creased and folded to become flexible. The finished model can be refolded to reveal different faces.

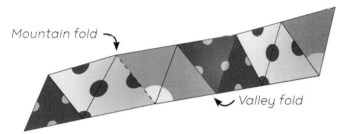

Mountain fold

Valley fold

Cut around the row of triangles, and fold the moutain and valley folds.

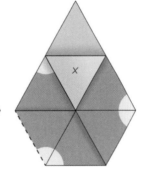

Flip the three triangles on the right to the back at the mountain fold.

Flip the three triangles on the left to the front on the valley fold.

Flip the grey triangle marked "x" here to the front.

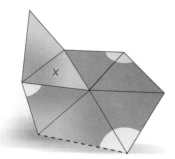

Glue the two grey triangles together.

Fold each triangle back and forth until the whole thing becomes really flexible.

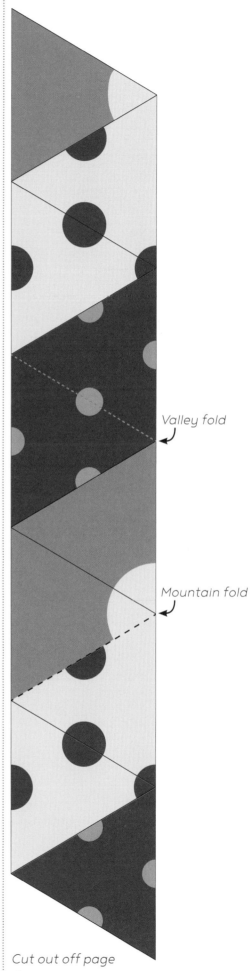

Valley fold

Mountain fold

Cut out off page

What happens?

Lift up two opposing triangles, and gently pull them upwards and outwards. This will take some practice and gets easier as the model limbers up. The faces of the object will turn and flip to reveal the six variations below:

Front

Back

Glue here

Glue here

Glue here

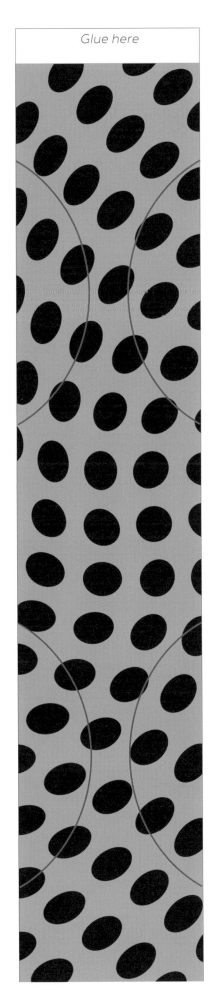

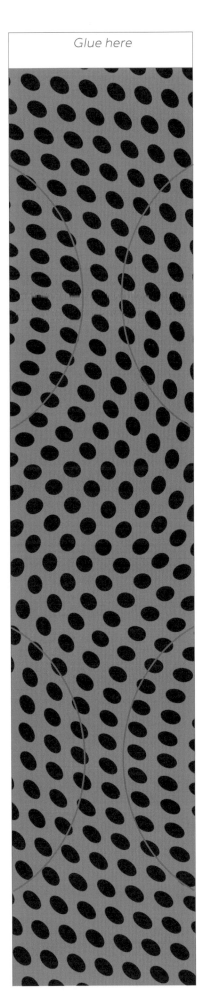

Score the pink lines.

Cut around the black line.

Glue here

Glue here

Glue here

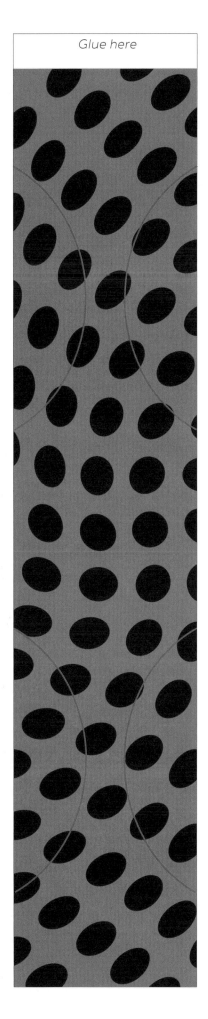

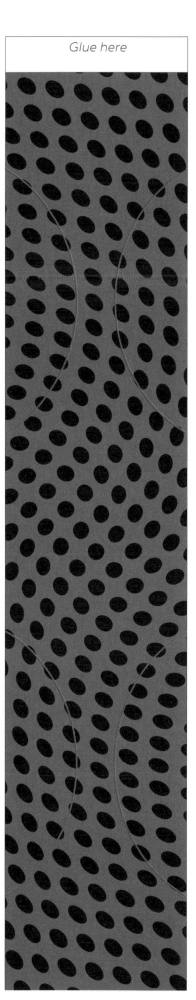

MAKE IT

Dotty Globe

These complex-looking globes are surprisingly simple to construct and the result is sturdy and fascinating to look at. The main trick when assembling the three pieces is to align the curves next to a straight bit of another strip. This is simple to do on the first two strips, but the third one will need turning.

1. Cut around the black outer lines - remember to include the white strip marked "Glue here".

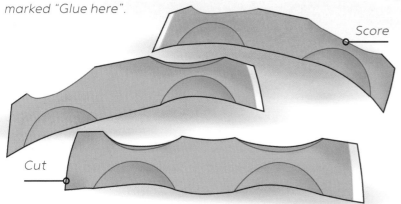

2. Choose which combination of colours you'd like and, with those sides facing up, lightly score the pink lines then gently crease them.

3. After creasing the pink lines, fold them back out flat as this makes it easier to assemble the globe.

4. Make a loop out of one piece by glueing in the white areas marked "Glue here".

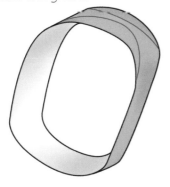

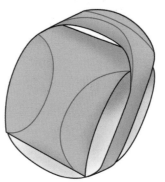

5. Make a second loop, then tuck it inside the first, at right-angles to it.

6. Make the third loop by threading it behind loop 2, but over loop 1 - see the picture on the left. Glue it after threading.

7. Turn loop three until all the scored half-circles are next to the place where the loops meet - check against the diagram on the left.

8. Pinch the pink crease lines to bend the semi-circles - this will lock the globe together.

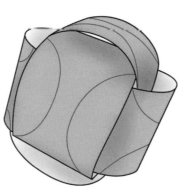

PUZZLE

Spot the Circles

Here are some circular close-ups – can you guess what they are? Answers are on page 94.

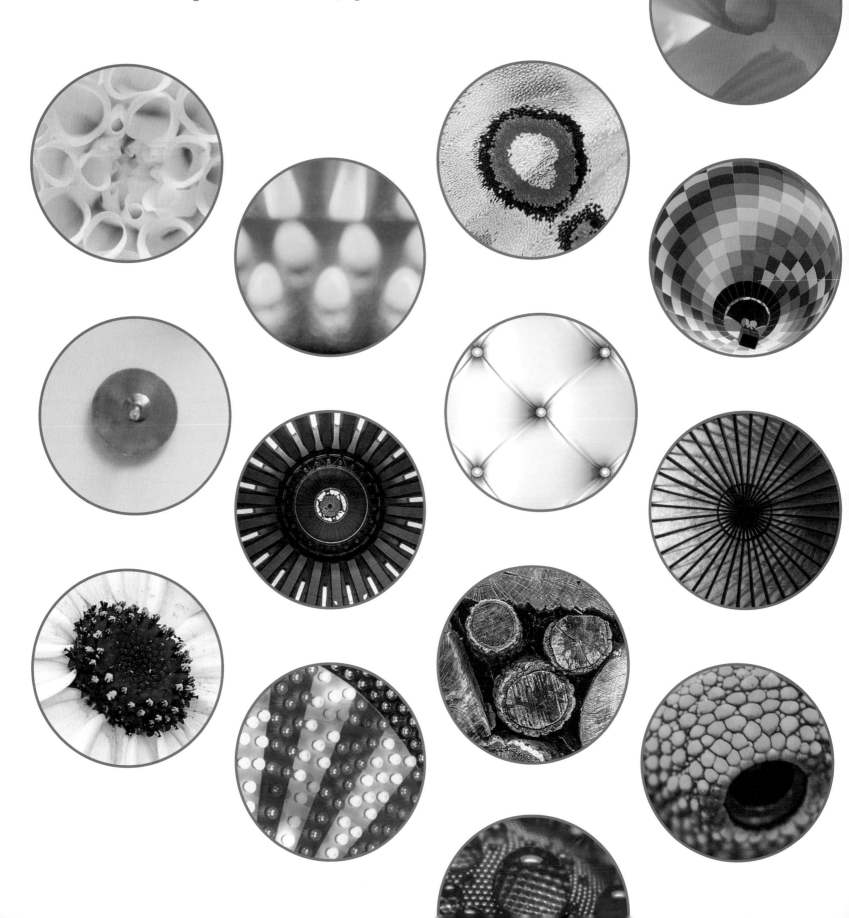

MAKE IT

Round Rosettes

Make these super-cute dotty rosettes. You will need some stick glue, cut string to hang them with and scissors.

1. Cut out each shape around the black line. Crease the dashed lines into mountain folds and the dotted lines to valley folds.

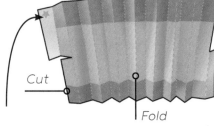

Cut

Fold

2. Place the piece so that the printed fold lines are on the top and the tab with the grey star is top left.

3. Pull the top and bottom towards each other and tuck the tab with the star to the back.

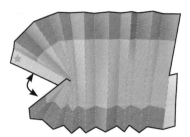

4. Glue the two blank tabs together, concentrating on just the outer edge - sliding them to align the tops nicely.

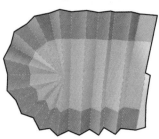

5. Flip it over and continue to glue along the whole length of the tab. A cocktail stick is handy for poking the glue into hard-to-reach areas.

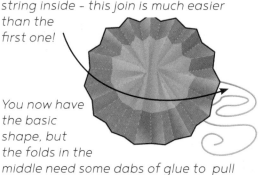

6. Glue the remaining two tabs together, sandwiching the end of your hanging string inside - this join is much easier than the first one!

You now have the basic shape, but the folds in the middle need some dabs of glue to pull the whole thing together and make more of a circle shape.

7. Put some tiny dabs of glue just in the centre to tack the tops of the folds together.

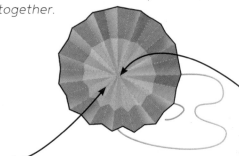

8. Then pinch together to form a circle.

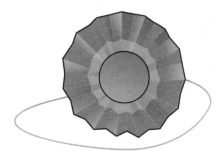

9. Choose a circle to cut out and stick to each side. Hang up and admire!

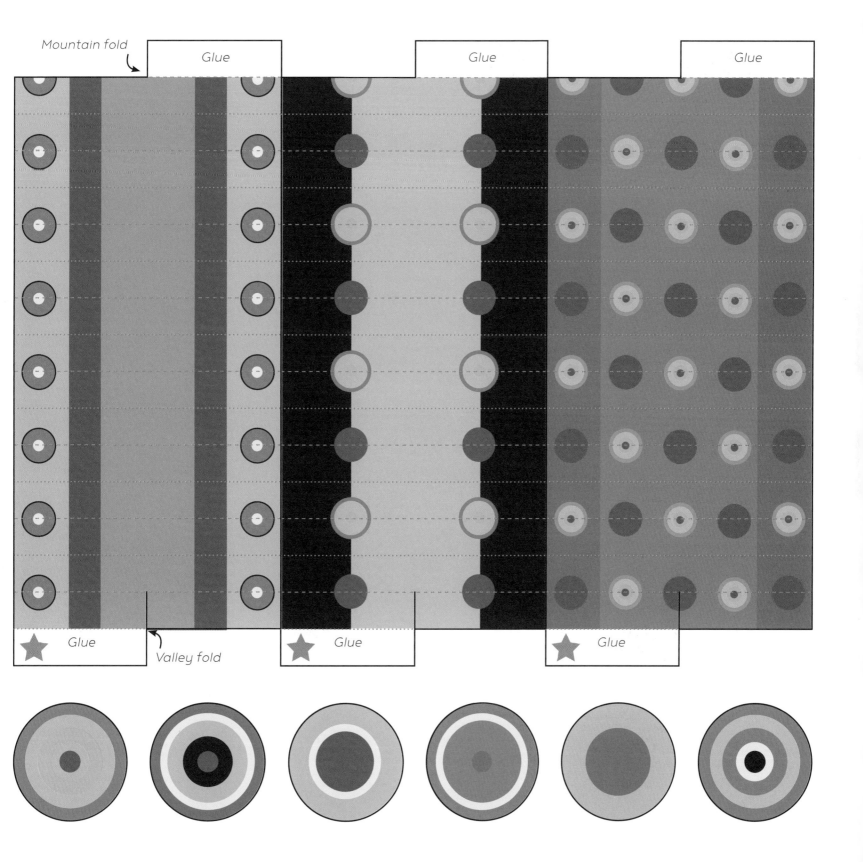

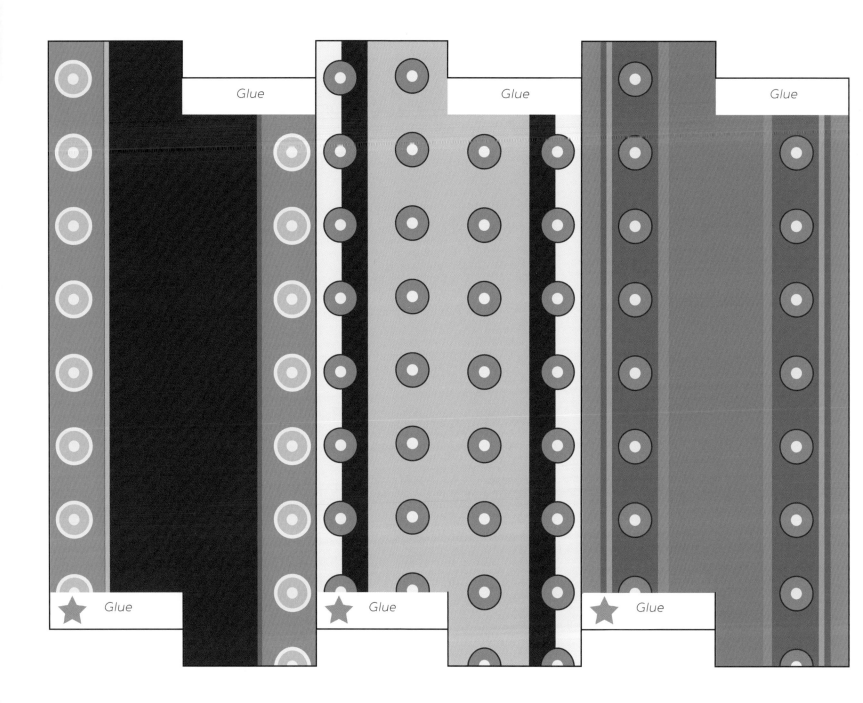

Glue

Glue

Glue

Glue

Glue

Glue

PUZZLE

Seeing Double

One of these splats appears twice – can you see which one? How long did it take?

Just can't see it? The answer is on page 95.

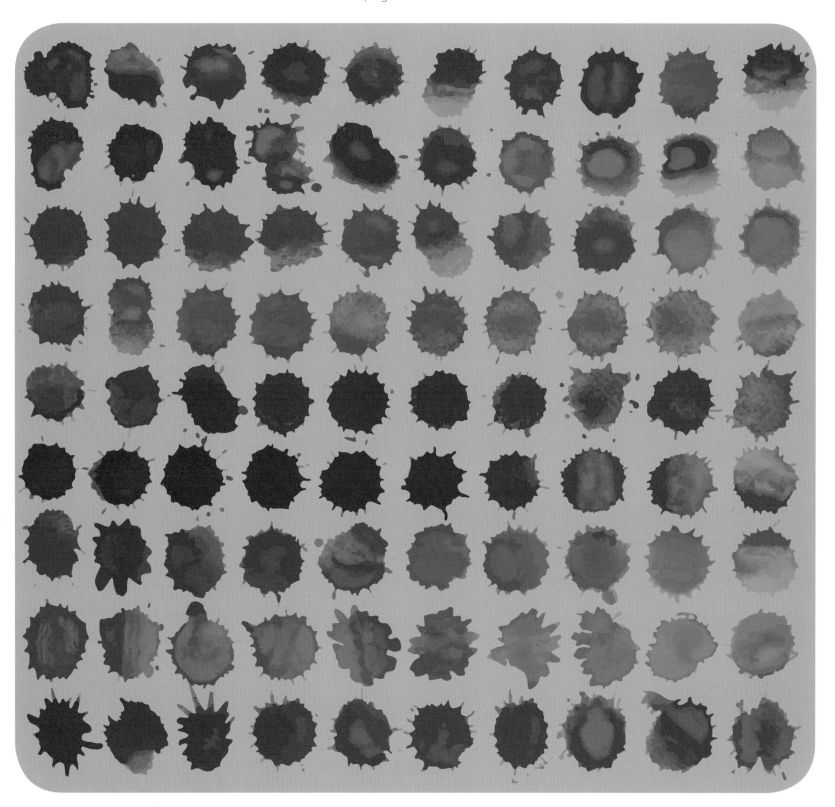

Dot the Difference

There are three differences in each picture on the right. See if you can spot them all. The solution is on page 95.

MAKE IT

Jelly Dots

This geometric shape is inspired by the experiments in paper cutting and folding that Josef Albers made at the Bauhaus nearly a hundred years ago.

It's amazing how it grows out of a flat piece of paper - the form and the way it wobbles makes it like a big paper jelly.

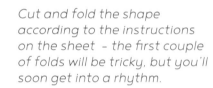

Cut and fold the shape according to the instructions on the sheet - the first couple of folds will be tricky, but you'll soon get into a rhythm.

The finished dot looks really good mounted on a wall over a constrasting colour - position it where you can be fascinated by the shadows it casts and the way the light falls on it.

This side is the back – you won't see these lines when you display and admire from the other side.

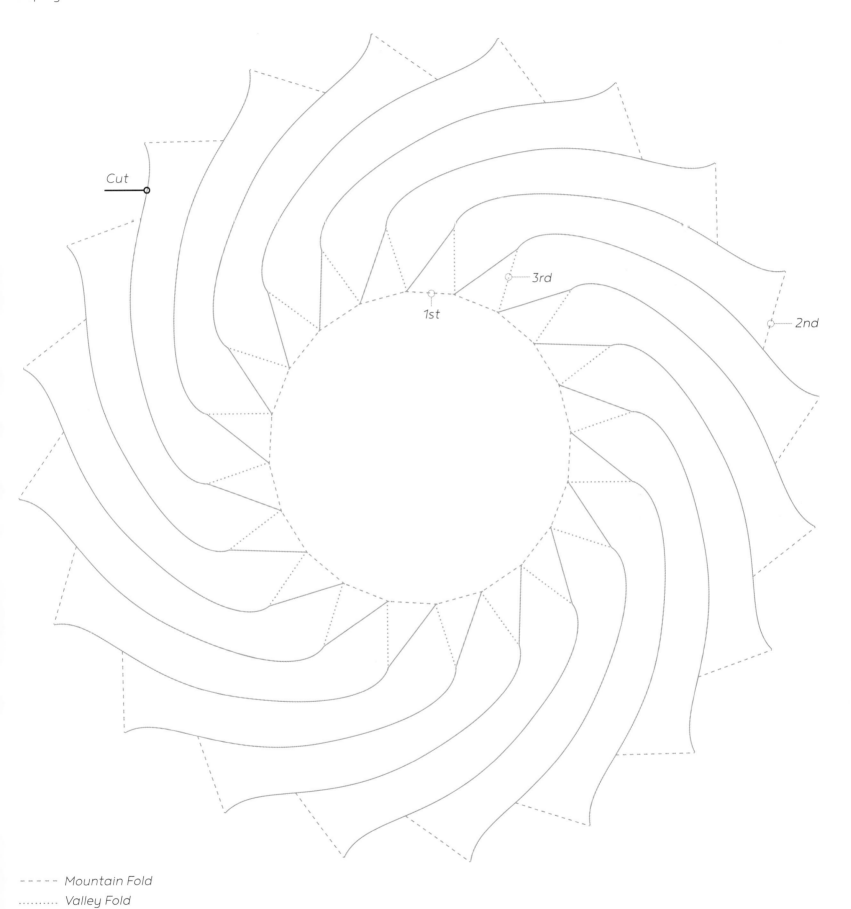

Cut

3rd

1st

2nd

- - - - Mountain Fold
.... Valley Fold

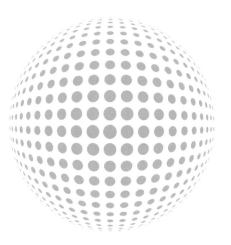

PUZZLE

Maze

Enter the maze by the red arrow and find your way to the red dot at the centre.

If you get lost, find the solution on page 96.

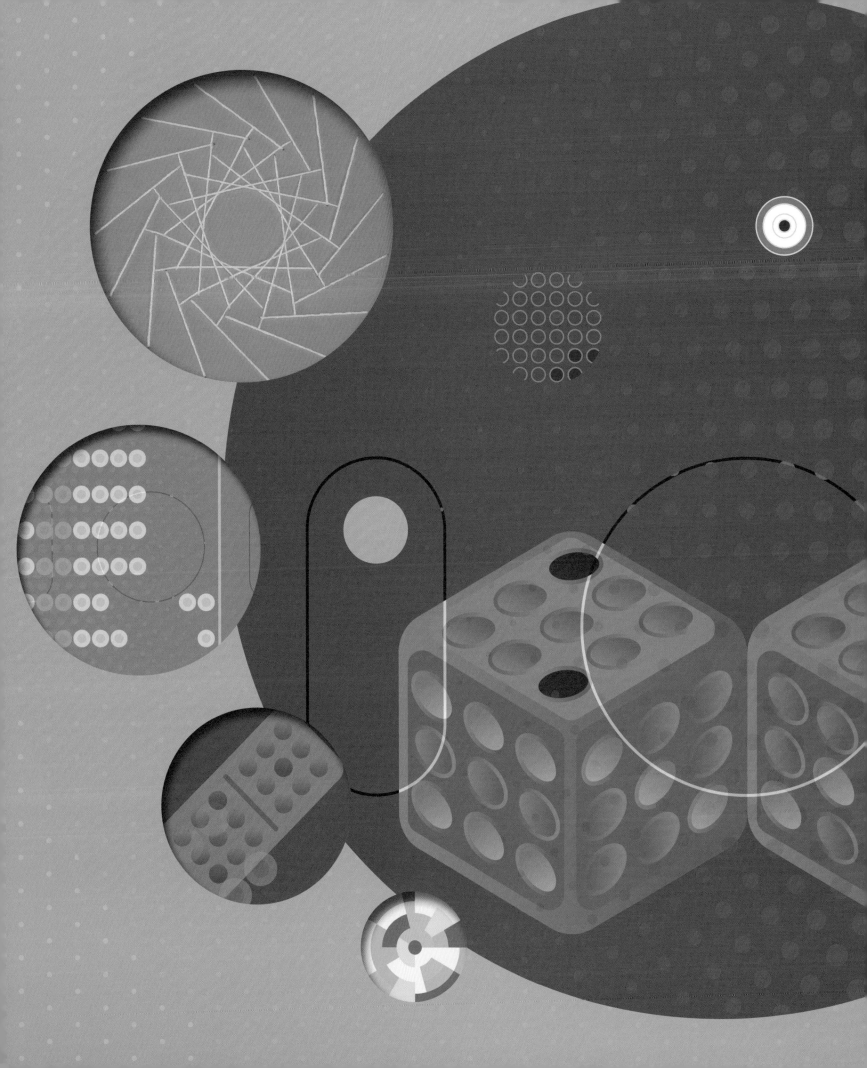

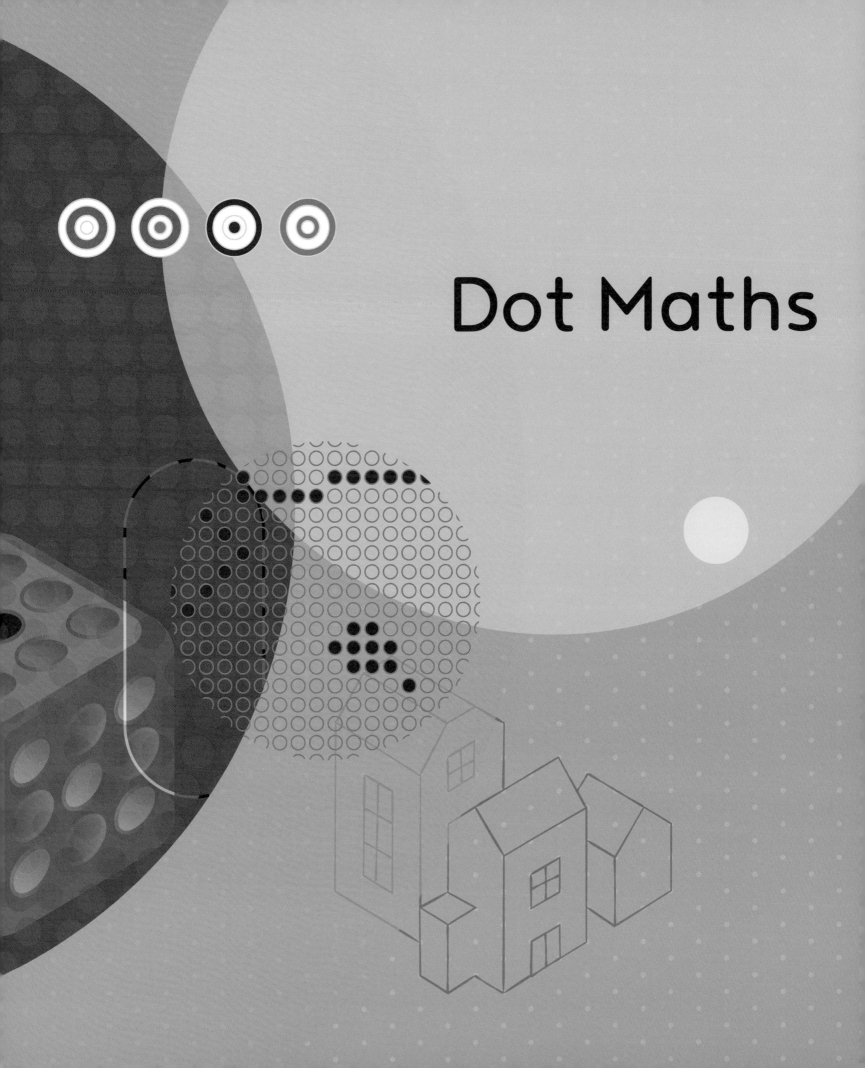

Dot Maths

ACTIVITY

The Art of Venn

Venn diagrams were invented by the English mathematician John Venn. They were first published in 1880 and showed the similarities and differences between sets of things. Think of some funny things the circles could contain. Things the circles have in common appear in the overlapping areas.

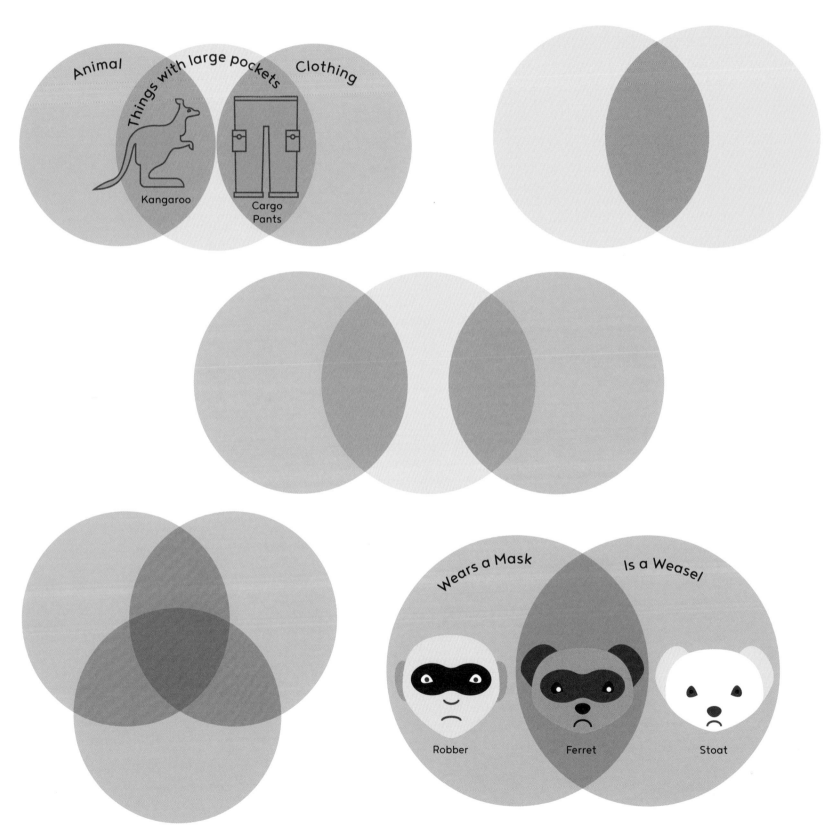

Animal

Things with large pockets

Clothing

Kangaroo

Cargo Pants

Wears a Mask

Is a Weasel

Robber

Ferret

Stoat

ART QUEST

Isometric City

These dots make an isometric grid - a grid that helps you to draw 3D objects without any perspective distortion. The elements in retro video games are often drawn using this method and Escher used it to create mind-bending landscapes. What will you draw? There are some doodled buildings to get you started.

PUZZLE

Scatter Art

Solve the sums below – the answers make a pair of co-ordinates - one for the X (across) and one for the Y (up and down). Make sure you do the multiplications (x) first. Colour the corresponding dot on the graph. The complete set of co-ordinates, when plotted, will make a picture. See the completed picture on page 96.

X:7+6, Y:6·5x4
X:25+10, Y:32
X:10·5x4, Y:68
X:2x8, Y: 12x4
X:17x2, Y:11
X:11x4, Y:51
X:11+18, Y:22x2
X:10·5x4, Y:56
X:16+18, Y:45
X:2x21, Y:3x7
X:17x2, Y:49
X:4x4, Y:35+14
X:17x2, Y: 50
X:40, Y:24x2
X:17·5x2, Y:17
X:21x2, Y:47
X:26+9, Y:22
X:8x2, Y:20x2·5
X:16+27, Y: 48
X:4x7, Y:(6x5)-1
X:38, Y:(2x9)+1
X:4x7, Y:8x5
X:16+27, Y:65
X:6x5·5, Y:47
X:39, Y:82-26
X:17x2, Y:18
X:4x7, Y:6+7
X:41, Y:56
X:7x4, Y:7x2
X:10·5x4, Y:20
X:4x7, Y:7+8
X:8x2, Y:12+39
X:27+16, Y:49
X:18+16, Y:33
X:13+16, Y:20+23
X:40, Y:49
X:5x6, Y: 2x3
X:2x21, Y:69
X:6x5, Y:3+4
X:8+8, Y:28+24
X:26+17, Y:3x22
X:16-3, Y:6x5
X:26+9, Y:47
X:4x4, Y:29+24
X:16+27, Y:67
X:13x2, Y:1x2
X:37, Y:20+14
X:2x13, Y:16x2
X:2x17, Y:32

X:41, Y:54
X:18+16, Y:36
X:36, Y:12x5
X:4x11, Y:50
X:16+18, Y:40
X:8+27, Y:36
X:2x13, Y:6x5
X:37, Y:17x2
X:13x2, Y:8x5
X:37, Y:17+26
X:4x4, Y:29+25
X:26+9, Y:30
X:40, Y: 9x5
X:17·5x2, Y:31
X:12+5, Y:3x1
X:13+16, Y:8x5
X:9+8, Y:8·5x4
X:41, Y:70
X:8+9, Y:17+21
X:17-4, Y:17+18
X:16+13, Y:6+6
X:37, Y:23x2
X:18+11, Y:9+9
X:27+8, Y:33
X:40, Y:24
X:17·5x2, Y:41
X:16+13, Y:20+22
X:11x3, Y:51
X:18-5, Y:(4x10)+1
X: 10-5, Y: 90-26
X:11-1, Y:3+7
X: 3+2, Y: (30x2)+2
X:5+5, Y:9+8
X:7+1, Y: (10x5)+6
X:9x3, Y:3x1
X: 11-7, Y: 6+45
X:3x9, Y:3+28
X:36, Y:63-4
X:3x9, Y: 8x5
X:10-2, Y: 100-46
X:16-5, Y:5x11
X:2x4, Y: 100-29
X:7x4, Y:8-5
X:40-30, Y:15
X:10-2, Y: 30+21
X:17-6, Y:15+28
X: 16-13, Y:60-2
X:13+16, Y:9x5
X:28+15, Y:57

X:7+3, Y:16x2
X: 2x1·5, Y: (10x5)+6
X:11+5, Y:6x5·5
X:37, Y:82-26
X:8+8, Y:3x13
X:4x4, Y:28+15
X:37, Y:28
X:2x8, Y:18+29
X: 15-12, Y:(10x6)+2
X:11-1, Y:11x3
X:10-7, Y: 48+13
X:37, Y:55-28
X:10x4·5, Y:11x5
X: 3x1, Y:6x10
X:2x5, Y:2x8
X:12+7, Y:13+28
X: 2+1, Y: 44+15
X:10-1, Y: 13·5x4
X:40, Y:27x2
X: 10-6, Y: 32x2
X:(2x5)+1, Y: 19+12
X:37, Y: 9+9
X: 2x2, Y: (6x10)+3
X:9x3 Y:6x5
X:2x5, Y: 4x3
X: 3+1, Y: 25+27
X:10x4·5, Y:54
X:6x2, Y:23x2
X:9x5, Y:59
X:6+13, Y:7x6
X:40, Y:82-26
X:26-7, Y:28+15
X:2x6, Y:18+8
X:12+7, Y:11x4
X:4x3, Y:21x2
X:2x23, Y:56
X: 1+11-9, Y:(5x10)+7
X:24/2, Y:12x3
X:6x6, Y:22
X:39, Y:27x2
X:12x3, Y:33
X:6x2, Y:6x5
X:10x4·5, Y:12x5
X:7+3, Y: 12x3
X: 4+1, Y: (30x2)+3
X:4x3, Y:5x5
X: 2·5x2, Y: 10x(6-1)
X:2x5, Y: 105/3
X:5x9, Y:61

X:24/2, Y:3+3
X:41, Y:(2x9)+1
X:15-2, Y: 2+4
X:10x4·5, Y:62
X:(6x2)-1, Y:4x9
X: 3x1, Y: (20x2·5)+5
X:44-34, Y: 12+32
X: 2+1, Y: 13·5x4
X:16x2, Y:39
X:5x3, Y:35+14
X:7+1, Y: (10x4)+6
X:24/2, Y:(11x5)+2
X:7+8, Y:11·5x4
X:5x9, Y:53
X:9+6, Y:8x5
X: 5x1, Y: (30x2)+6
X:6x6, Y:21
X:3x5, Y:8·5x4
X: 3x1, Y: (10X5)+3
X:(9x5)+1, Y:58
X: 2x2, Y: 20+45
X:7+3, Y:6·5x2
X:4+4, Y: 10x5
X:17·5x2, Y:24x2
X:38, Y:37
X:12x3, Y:17
X:2x4, Y: 23+26
X:7+3, Y: 23·5x2
X:3x3, Y: (10x5)+6
X:8+7, Y:28+15
X: 10-5, Y: 58+3
X:40-30, Y:4+7
X:5x4, Y:2+1
X: 4+1, Y: 10x6
X:3·5x4, Y:13+28
X:38, Y:12x3
X: 10-5, Y: 50+9
X:3x3, Y: 9x5
X:3x12, Y:29
X: 3+2, Y: 50+8
X:7x2, Y:3x9
X:2x7, Y: 4x7
X: 5x5, Y:16x2
X:5+9, Y:6x5
X:4+28, Y: 54
X:38, Y:35
X:11x3, Y:18
X:41, Y:51
X:6x5·5, Y: 37

X:6+8, Y:7x5
X:17-6, Y:(9x2)+1
X:4x5, Y:6·5x6
X:(2x5)+1, Y:4x2
X:38, Y:13+13
X:15-4, Y:4+3
X:9+4, Y:12x5
X:41, Y:100/2
X:3·5x4, Y: 3+2
X:3x4, Y:23+36
X:41, Y:26x2
X:4x3, Y:(11x5)+1
X:3+3, Y: 34+33
X:13+16, Y: 2x2
X: 5, Y: 49+8
X:41, Y: 80-27
X: 10-5, Y: 35+14
X:15-4, Y:18+4
X:52-35, Y:28+15
X: 2x3, Y: 23+37+9
X:4x7, Y:9+8
X:10-1, Y: 12x4
X:10-4, Y: 34x2
X:16-5, Y:3x7
X:38, Y:9+9
X:16+13, Y:10-5
X:17-6, Y:18+5
X:17-12, Y: 33+33
X:2x5, Y:2x7
X:3x8, Y:8x5
X:3+3, Y: 32·5x2
X:38, Y:20+18
X:10-4, Y: (10x5)+6
X:18+4, Y:6-4
X:2x5, Y: 16+38
X:2x3, Y: 24x2
X:9+4, Y:18+29
X:46, Y:72-14
X:5+8, Y:14·5x4
X: 50/2, Y:3+28
X:41, Y:23
X: 50/2, Y:5-3
X:6+7, Y:26+33
X:3+4, Y: 35x2
X:3x6, Y:10-7
X:8x3, Y:3+28
X:41, Y:(9x5)+1
X: 5x5, Y:8x5

X:6x3, Y: 7x5
X:10+9, Y:9x5
X:6x3, Y: 18+19
X:7x3, Y:2+1
X:3x6, Y:11x4
X:10-3, Y: 80-11
X:15-4, Y:14·5x4
X:3x5, Y:12+39
X:4x11, Y:64
X:5+2, Y: (10x6)+8
X:2x5, Y:7+2
X:2x7, Y: 11x4
X:11x4, Y:63
X:8+6, Y: 9x5
X:7x4, Y:8+8
X:5·5x8, Y:59
X:17+12, Y:6+5
X:4x11, Y:12x5
X:7x2, Y:19+29
X:5·5x8, Y:58
X:6+9, Y:20x2·5
X:5+2, Y: (10x5)+6
X:7+3, Y:27+7
X:6x5, Y:40
X:10-3, Y: 30+24
X:11x4, Y:62
X:3x7, Y:6·5x6
X:5+5, Y: 19x3
X:16x2, Y:19
X:36, Y:72-14
X:3+4, Y: 20+33
X:32, Y:53
X:6+9, Y:(2x10)+9
X:4+18, Y:6·5x6
X:5x6, Y:45
X:36, Y:23x2
X:6x5, Y:46
X:5·5x8, Y: 61
X:20+11, Y:19
X:2x11·5, Y:(6x5)+9
X:36, Y:60-3
X:2x16, Y:49
X:3x8, Y: 7-5
X:39, Y:47
X:11x3, Y:46
X:38, Y:23x2
X:5x3, Y:2x2
X:38, Y: 60-3
X:5+11, Y:3+1

Y

X:3+4, Y: 24+23
X:6+26, Y:48
X:6x5, Y:2x4
X:39, Y:(2x9)+1
X:5x6, Y:3x3
X:21+10, Y:38
X:36, Y:21x2
X:22+9, Y:43
X:11·5x2, Y:26–24
X:31–19, Y:57
X:4+28, Y:37
X:39, Y:50/2
X:5+27, Y: 43
X:6x5, Y:5+5
X:41, Y:5·5x4
X:12+7, Y: 3x1
X:6x5·5, Y:43
X:19, Y:12x3
X:9x5, Y:52
X:38, Y:29+26
X:3+29, Y:50
X:37, Y:63–4
X:5x6, Y:44
X:26–7, Y:3x13
X:39, Y:5·5x8
X:5x6, Y:8+11
X:13+6, Y:8x5
X:16x2, Y:51
X:36, Y: 50–13
X:4+28, Y:52
X:38, Y:17+26
X:5+5, Y:2x4
X:6x5·5, Y:40
X:38, Y:39
X:15–4, Y:23x2
X:3x10, Y: 41
X:88–83, Y: 22x3
X:10x·5, Y: 137 – 70
X: (4x3)–1, Y: 12x2
X: 30–4, Y: 30+1
X: 14+21, Y: (6x7)+5
X: 75–29, Y: 33+24

X

MAKE IT

Puzzle and Spinner

Concentric Circle Puzzle

Cut out this puzzle, mess it up, then put it back together again... without going dotty!

Fearsome geometry - the puzzle is designed around concentric circles that are intersected by varying radii.

The solution is on page 96.

Analogue to Die for

Popping a pencil into the middle of the spinner makes an analogue die: the circular shape of this spinner means that it can land at any point between numbers 1-12... Cutting straight edges, and so causing it to land on a definitive edge, would make it digital as it would land either on or off a number, with no in-between stages.

Cut around the black dotted lines.

String Theory – parts one and two

For both these projects, sew between the dots in numerical order. A good thread to use is embroidery "silk" as it's good and chunky, and the way it's braided means it grips the holes without snagging and catching. Don't split the thread – use all six strands at once.

MAKE IT

Cut along the black dotted lines.

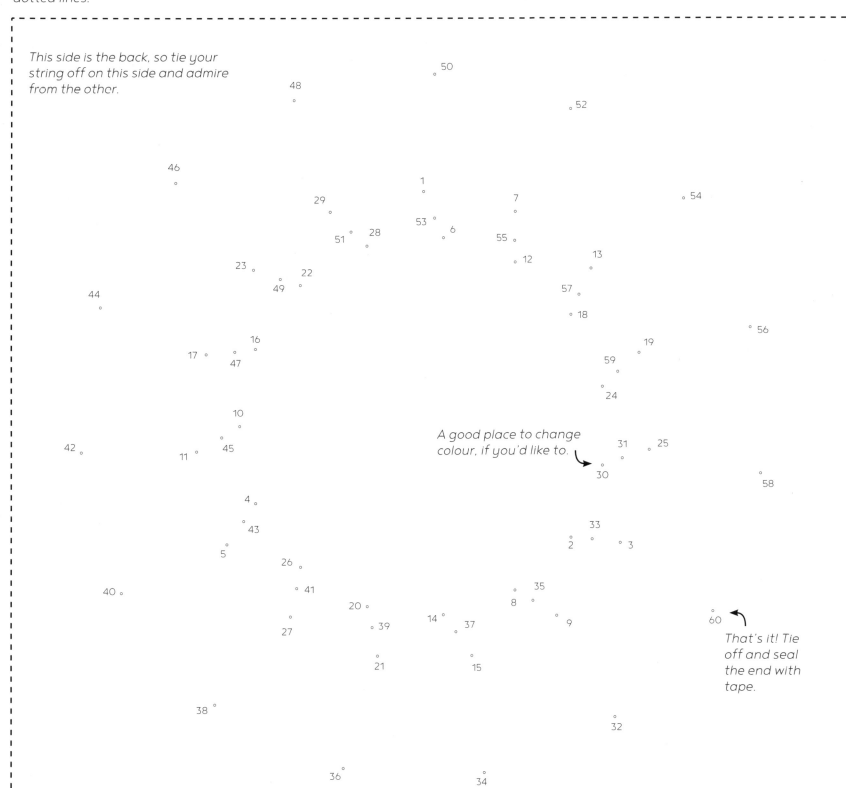

This side is the back, so tie your string off on this side and admire from the other.

A good place to change colour, if you'd like to.

That's it! Tie off and seal the end with tape.

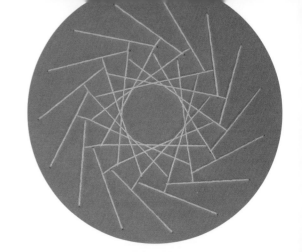

Think about which colour silk you will use on these projects – embroidery silk comes in a vast array of colours. Will it be darker or lighter than the background colour? Will it tone or contrast? Will you use two colours - or more?

TIP: The tension of the string is key – there needs to be enough tension to make the lines straight without bending the card. In the second project, you'll need to check that the tension of the second thread is the same as the first. There are larger finished examples of this and the next piece in the Solutions section, page 96.

65 64 61 60 57 56 53 52 49 48 45 44 41 40 37 36 33 32 29 28

25 24 21 20 17 16 13 12 9 8 5 4 1

Mountain Fold

2 3 6 7 10 11 14 15 18 19 22 23 26 62 63 66 59 58 55 54 51 50 47 46 43 42 39 38 35 34 31 30 27

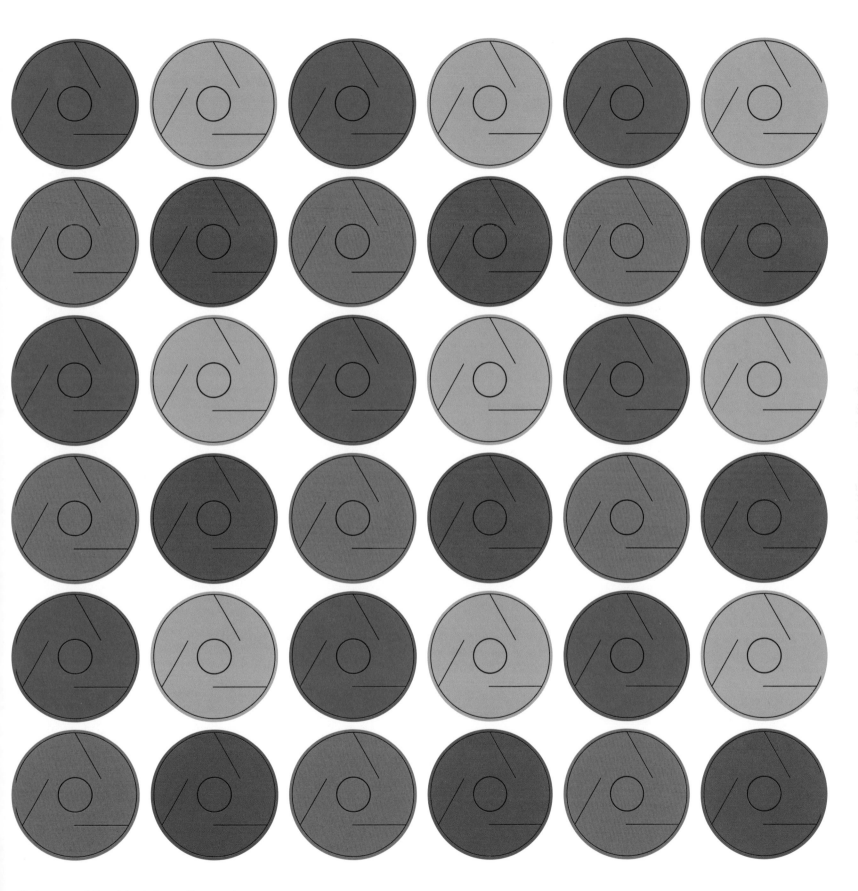

Cut around the black lines. To create more
globe shades, scan the page before cutting.

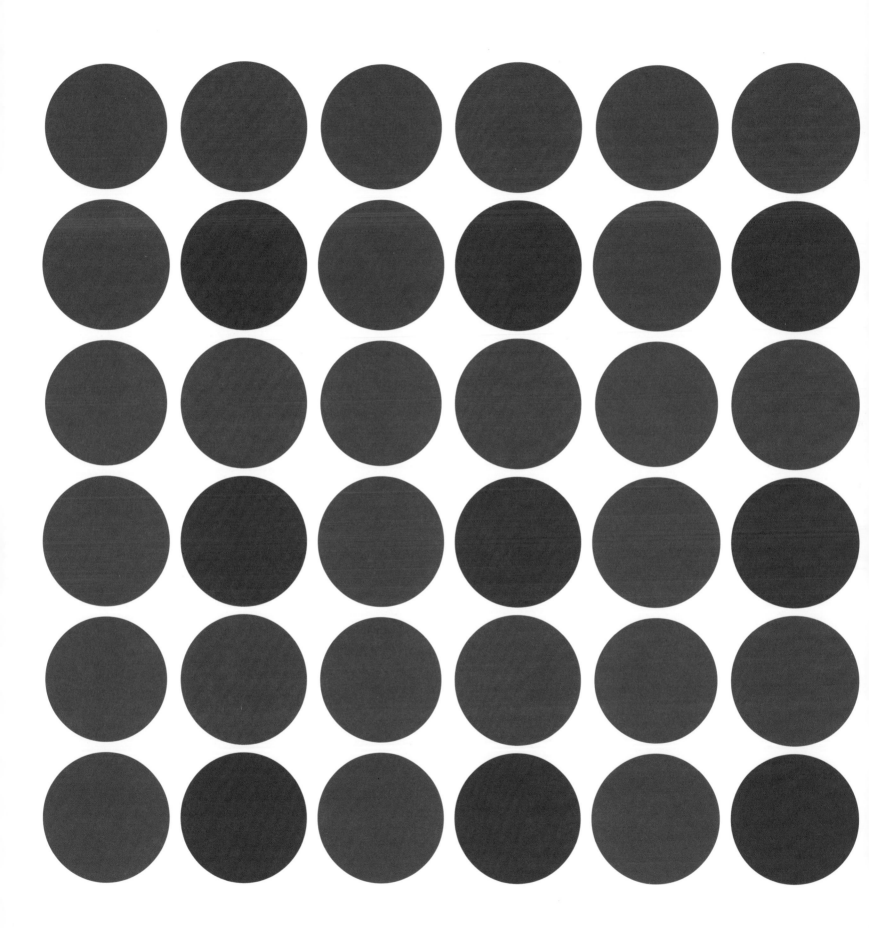

MAKE IT

Light and Shade

In the middle of the last century, Richard Buckminster Fuller, architect and designer, experimented with structures formed with equilateral triangles. An equilateral triangle cut into a dot is what we are using for this project.

Three pieces are joined at each corner, but it's possible to join up to six circles at each corner – have a play!

In the photograph, you can see that pieces of coloured translucent paper have been stuck over the "windows" of each piece – they look great when illuminated by the fairy lights.

There are enough cut-out pieces to make nine globe shades. If you'd like to make more, scan and print the page before you start.

Note that the dots have a front and a back. Each globe can be made with either the front or the back facing out, but they all have to match within the globe itself.

1. This is how the dots slot together.

2. To make the globes, three dots are slotted at each corner – a finished corner will look like this.

3. When you make each globe, slot the four dots together loosely, like this:

4. Then pull each dot gently to close the globe.

5. Pop a fairy light into the opening of one of the corners of each globe. The tension in the globe should mean they will sit in place quite happily without glue.

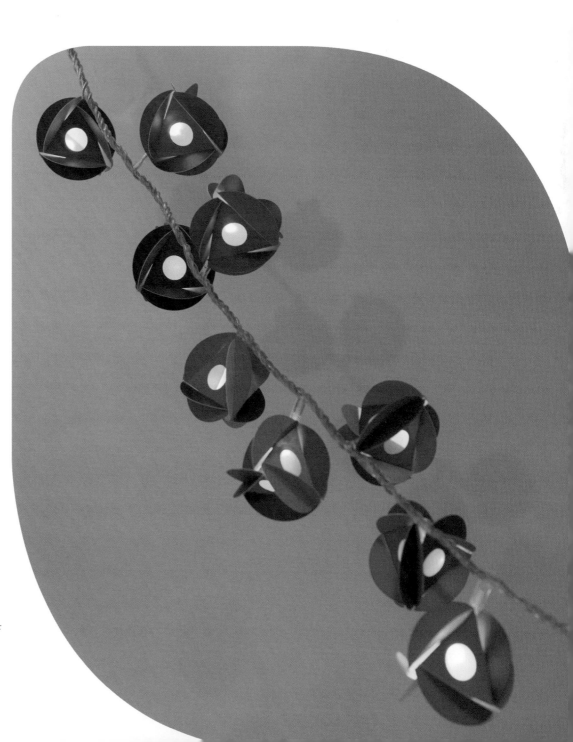

PUZZLE

SuDotku

Only one of each type of dot in each set of nine, and only one type of dot in each row and column. You will need a black, a blue and a red pen ... and maybe some correction fluid.

Boggled? The solution is on page 96.

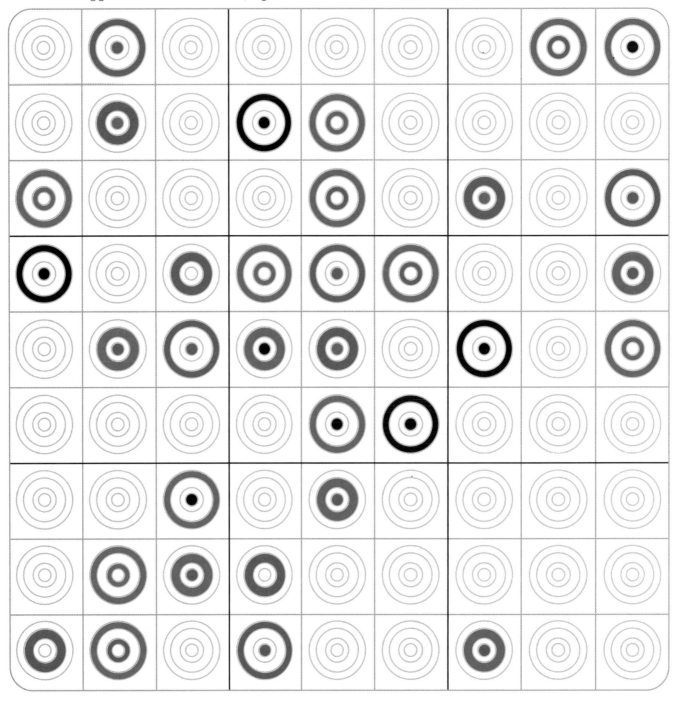

Solutions

Solutions

Here you will find the solutions to all the problems.

Page 33
Albert Einstein

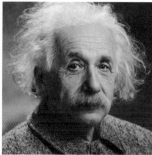

Page 24
Colour Wheel

Page 25
Stand Well Back

Page 35 Cloud Tones

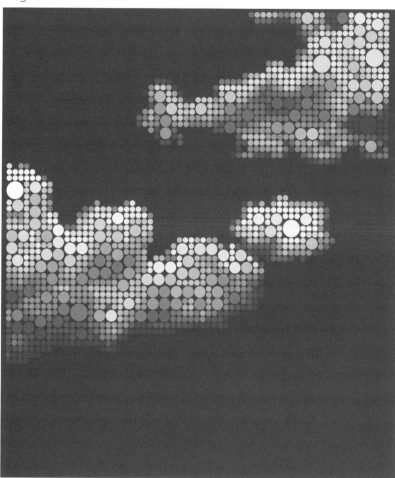

Page 40 Circular Logic

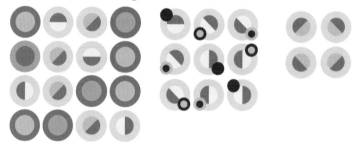

Page 41
Numberless Dot2Dot

Page 47 Spherical Scene

Page 49 Colour Me Kahlo

Page 62 Spot the Circles - down in columns from left to right

Dahlia from above

Items of stationery

Anenomes

Gas cooker ring

Dome from below

Fairground lights

Apollo butterfly

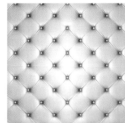

Button-backed board

Wood pile

Insect eye

Pasta

Hot air balloon from below

Japanese paper umbrella

Chameleon

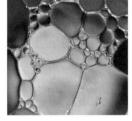

Bubbles

Seed head

Cheetah

White currants

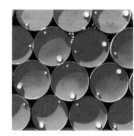

Pearl-spotted owl

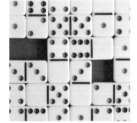

Liquid storage containers

Bubbles

Dominoes

Dartboard

Peacock

Clockwork mechanism

Ladybird in the rain

Manual typewriter

Cycle wheel

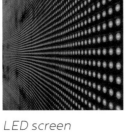

LED screen

Silk lanterns

Page 67 Seeing Double

Pages 68–69 Dot the Difference

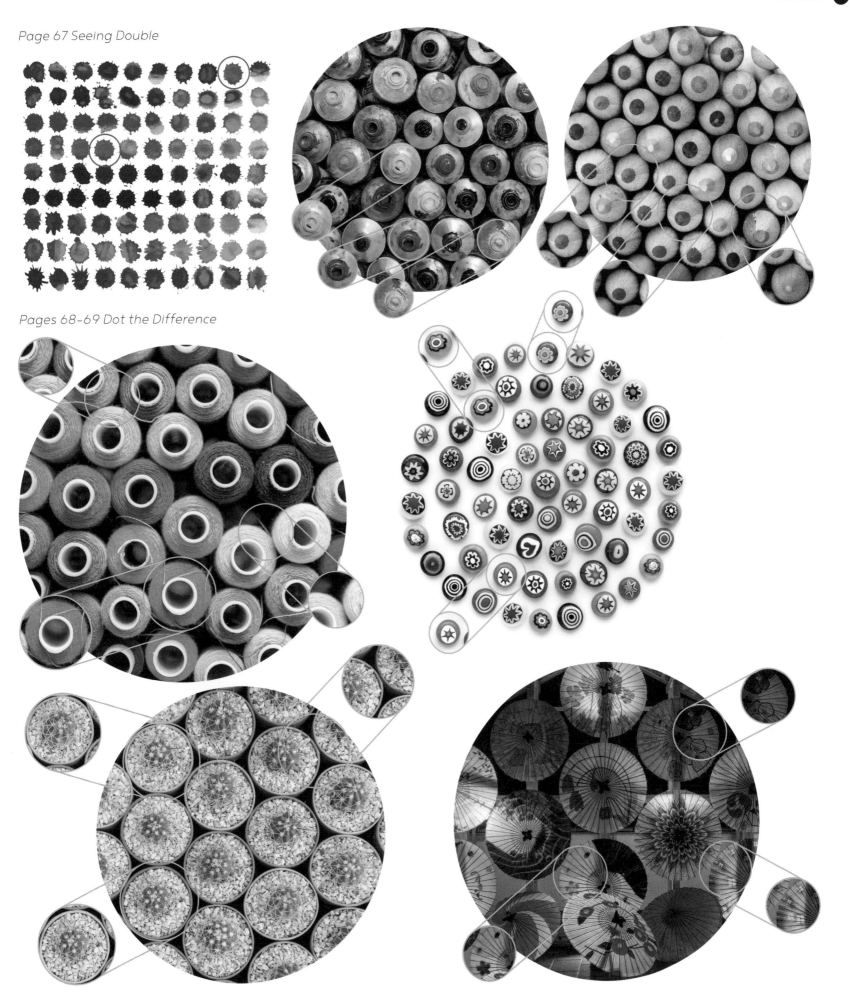

Page 73
Maze

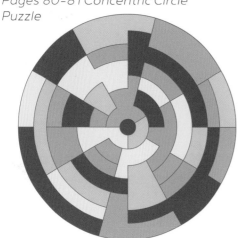

Pages 80–81 Concentric Circle Puzzle

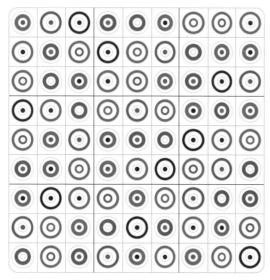

Page 90 SuDotku

Pages 78–79 Scatter Art

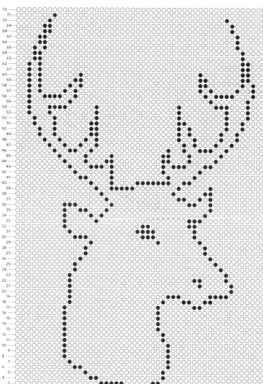

Pages 84–87 String Theory

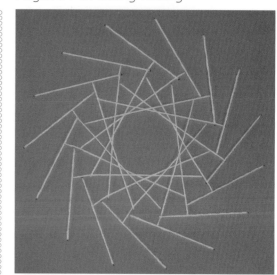

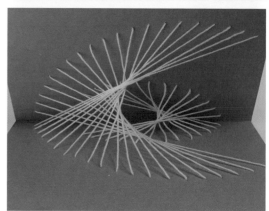

Picture credits

The publishers would like to thank the following sources for their kind permission to reproduce the pictures in this book.

(Key: t = top, b = bottom, c = centre, l = left & r = right)

Alamy: 9 , 13, 21; /Pexels: 3, 4, 5(tr), 10(t), 14(m), 22, 34, 36(b), 55(b), 62–63, 68(tr), 68(br); /Rex Features by Shutterstock: 10(b); /Shutterstock: 6, 11(b), 14(t), 15(t), 15(l), 15(m), 15(r), 40, 43(t), 43(m), 44–45, 54(tl), 54(l), 67, 68(t), 68(tl), 68(bl), 68(m), 68(mr), 72–73; /MCCRAFT: 14(b); /Wikimedia Commons: 33

Every effort has been made to acknowledge correctly and contact the source and/or copyright holder of each picture and Carlton Books Limited apologises for any unintentional errors or omissions, which will be corrected in future editions of this book.

References
Pages 57–58: trihexaflexagon invented by Arthur H Stone.
Pages 70–73: structure inspired by Josef Albers and Prof Yoshinobu Minamoto.
Page 89: thanks to Paul Jackson, *Cut and Fold Techniques for Designers*.